Prime Ministers and Party Governments in Central and Eastern Europe

This book focuses on Prime Ministers (PMs) in the post-communist democracies of Central and Eastern Europe (CEE). It shows how the survival of PMs in chief executive office depends on their interrelations with other actors in three different arenas. The first arena encompasses the linkages between PMs and their parties. In this respect, being a party leader is a major power resource for PMs to retain office even under critical circumstances. At the heart of the second arena is the PMs' relationship to other parliamentary parties. In this regard, the high fragmentation and fluidity of many post-communist party systems pose enormous challenges for PMs to secure constant parliamentary support. In the third arena, PMs are confronted with state presidents. Given their relatively strong powers in most CEE countries, presidents may use their constitutional powers to interfere in the political domain of PMs and thus jeopardise the stability of party governments. This book offers new evidence on these relationships from case studies and a broader comparative perspective.

This volume will be of great use to students and researchers interested in comparative politics and government, European studies, and political leadership. The chapters in this book were originally published as a special issue of *East European Politics* and are accompanied by a revised introduction and a new conclusion.

Florian Grotz is Professor of Comparative Government at Helmut Schmidt University, Hamburg, Germany.

Marko Kukec is Post-doctoral Researcher at Helmut Schmidt University, Hamburg, Germany.

Prime Ministers and Party Governments in Central and Eastern Europe

**Edited by
Florian Grotz and Marko Kukec**

LONDON AND NEW YORK

First published 2024
by Routledge
4 Park Square, Milton Park, Abingdon, Oxon, OX14 4RN

and by Routledge
605 Third Avenue, New York, NY 10158

Routledge is an imprint of the Taylor & Francis Group, an informa business

Introduction © 2024 Florian Grotz and Marko Kukec
Conclusion © 2024 Marko Kukec and Florian Grotz
Chapters 1, 4 and 5 © 2024 Taylor & Francis
Chapter 2 © 2021 Maria Spirova and Radostina Sharenkova-Toshkova. Originally published as Open Access.
Chapter 3 © 2021 Daniel Kovarek. Originally published as Open Access.

With the exception of Chapters 2 and 3, no part of this book may be reprinted or reproduced or utilised in any form or by any electronic, mechanical, or other means, now known or hereafter invented, including photocopying and recording, or in any information storage or retrieval system, without permission in writing from the publishers. For details on the rights for Chapters 2 and 3, please see the chapters' Open Access footnotes.

Trademark notice: Product or corporate names may be trademarks or registered trademarks, and are used only for identification and explanation without intent to infringe.

British Library Cataloguing-in-Publication Data
A catalogue record for this book is available from the British Library

ISBN13: 978-1-032-51970-8 (hbk)
ISBN13: 978-1-032-51971-5 (pbk)
ISBN13: 978-1-003-40469-9 (ebk)

DOI: 10.4324/9781003404699

Typeset in Myriad Pro
by codeMantra

Publisher's Note
The publisher accepts responsibility for any inconsistencies that may have arisen during the conversion of this book from journal articles to book chapters, namely the inclusion of journal terminology.

Disclaimer
Every effort has been made to contact copyright holders for their permission to reprint material in this book. The publishers would be grateful to hear from any copyright holder who is not here acknowledged and will undertake to rectify any errors or omissions in future editions of this book.

Contents

Citation Information	vi
Notes on Contributors	vii

Introduction

The survival of prime ministers in Central and Eastern European party governments   1
Florian Grotz and Marko Kukec

1   Coping with the new party challenge: patterns of prime ministerial survival in Croatia and Slovenia   20
Dario Nikić Čakar and Alenka Krašovec

2   Juggling friends and foes: Prime Minister Borissov's surprise survival in Bulgaria   35
Maria Spirova and Radostina Sharenkova-Toshkova

3   Prime ministers in minority governments: the case of Hungary   51
Daniel Kovarek

4   Prime ministers, presidents and ministerial selection in Lithuania   69
Lukas Pukelis and Mažvydas Jastramskis

5   Puppets of the president? Prime ministers in post-communist Romania   84
Laurenţiu Ştefan

Conclusion

Weak chief executives? Post-communist prime ministers between their parties, parliaments and presidents   99
Marko Kukec and Florian Grotz

Index   107

Citation Information

The following chapters were originally published in the journal *East European Politics*, volume 37, issue 3 (2021). When citing this material, please use the original page numbering for each article, as follows:

Chapter 1
Coping with the new party challenge: patterns of prime ministerial survival in Croatia and Slovenia
Dario Nikić Čakar and Alenka Krašovec
East European Politics, volume 37, issue 3 (2021) pp. 417–431

Chapter 2
Juggling friends and foes: Prime Minister Borissov's surprise survival in Bulgaria
Maria Spirova and Radostina Sharenkova-Toshkova
East European Politics, volume 37, issue 3 (2021) pp. 432–447

Chapter 3
Prime ministers in minority governments: the case of Hungary
Daniel Kovarek
East European Politics, volume 37, issue 3 (2021) pp. 448–465

Chapter 4
Prime ministers, presidents and ministerial selection in Lithuania
Lukas Pukelis and Mažvydas Jastramskis
East European Politics, volume 37, issue 3 (2021) pp. 466–480

Chapter 5
Puppets of the president? Prime ministers in post-communist Romania
Laurențiu Ștefan
East European Politics, volume 37, issue 3 (2021) pp. 481–495

For any permission-related enquiries please visit:
http://www.tandfonline.com/page/help/permissions

Notes on Contributors

Florian Grotz is Professor of Comparative Government at Helmut Schmidt University, Hamburg, Germany.

Mažvydas Jastramskis is Assistant Professor in the Institute of International Relations and Political Science (IIRPS) at Vilnius University, Lithuania.

Daniel Kovarek is a PhD candidate at Central European University, Vienna, Austria.

Alenka Krašovec is Professor of Political Science at the Faculty of Social Sciences at the University of Ljubljana, Slovenia.

Marko Kukec is Post-doctoral Researcher at Helmut Schmidt University, Hamburg, Germany.

Dario Nikić Čakar is Assistant Professor of Comparative Politics at the Faculty of Political Science at the University of Zagreb, Croatia.

Lukas Pukelis is a lead data scientist at Public Policy and Management Institute, Vilnius, Lithuania.

Radostina Sharenkova-Toshkova teaches Politics of Memory at the Institute of Political Science at Leiden University, Netherlands.

Maria Spirova is Associate Professor of Comparative Politics and International Relations at the Institute of Political Science at Leiden University, Netherlands.

Laurenţiu Ştefan is Senior Researcher at the Center for Public Policies at the West University of Timişoara, Romania, and Associate Lecturer at the major faculties of Political Science across the country (National School for Political and Administrative Studies – Bucharest, University of Bucharest, Babeş-Bolyai University of Cluj-Napoca, and West University of Timişoara).

INTRODUCTION

The survival of prime ministers in Central and Eastern European party governments

Florian Grotz ⑩ and Marko Kukec ⑩

This article is the introduction to the volume on Prime Ministers (PMs) and party governments in CEE. It argues that the political survival of PMs in post-communist democracies depends on their interrelationships with other actors in three different arenas. The first arena encompasses the linkages between PMs and their parties. In this respect, being a party leader is a major power resource for PMs to retain their office even under critical circumstances. At the heart of the second arena is the PMs' relationship to other parliamentary parties. In this regard, the high fragmentation and fluidity of many post-communist party systems pose enormous challenges for PMs to secure constant parliamentary support. In the third arena, PMs are confronted with state presidents. Relatively strong CEE presidents, especially in semi-presidential systems, may use their constitutional powers to interfere in the political domain of PMs and thus jeopardize the stability of party governments. For each of these interrelationships, this article provides systematic evidence for eleven CEE democracies from 1990 to 2019.

Prime ministers in post-communist democracies

Stable and effective party governments are essential for making parliamentary democracy work. In this regard, Prime Ministers (PMs) play a key role because their political leadership as chief executives has a decisive impact on the stability and effectiveness of their governments (King 1975; Strangio, 't Hart, and Walter 2013). Therefore, the comparative study of party government usually takes the replacement of PM among the defining criteria for cabinet duration, on a par with changes in the partisan composition of government and general elections (King et al. 1990). Moreover, research on parliamentary democracies in Western countries has shown that the political significance of PMs has further increased over the last decades, given the ongoing internationalization of politics, personalization of political communication and weakening of cleavage structures (Poguntke and Webb 2005, 13–17).

In the parliamentary democracies of CEE, the situation seems to be more ambiguous. An early study on PMs in post-communist democracies contends that they have been significantly shorter in office than their Western counterparts (Baylis 2007, 81). This impression is challenged in a more recent study, pointing to the growing prominence of PMs in some CEE countries, which seem to follow the path of "presidentialization" identified in Western Europe before (Hloušek 2015). Finally, a broader comparative inspection reveals that the tenure of PMs in CEE considerably differs across and within individual countries (Grotz and Weber 2017).

The reasons for this intriguing variation of prime-ministerial survival in post-communist democracies have not been sufficiently explored. Baylis (2007) attributes the "prime ministerial weakness" in CEE to various specificities of the post-communist context, such as party system instability, powerful state presidents, inexperience of political elites and policy constraints caused by economic transformation and Europeanization, but does not systematically explore these arguments in empirical perspective. Needless to say, there are several analyses on the stability of post-communist party governments (Grotz and Weber 2012; Tzelgov 2011; Schleiter and Morgan-Jones 2009). Likewise, quite a few studies have dealt with cabinet members and cabinet decision-making in CEE democracies (Blondel and Müller-Rommel 2001; Blondel, Müller-Rommel, and Malová 2007; Fettelschoss and Nikolenyi 2008). However, we know surprisingly little about why some PMs in CEE succeeded to stay significantly longer in chief executive office than others.

This book seeks to answer this question by qualitative case studies that are embedded in a common theoretical framework. The following contributions focus on selected PMs from different CEE countries and investigate their interactions with other key political players. In doing so, they shed light on how PMs succeeded to organize support of their allies, prevail in conflicts with their main political rivals, and elaborate on the factors that explain their different survival in office.

This chapter provides a systematic overview of prime-ministerial duration in the eleven EU member countries of CEE and situates the following contributions of the book within a broader comparative perspective. We proceed with a theoretical framework, which places PMs within their party governments, and elaborate on their interrelationships with other political actors in three arenas that are crucial for their survival in office: their own party, other parliamentary parties and the state president. Afterwards, we explore the patterns of prime-ministerial duration with respect to these arenas, by concentrating on individual and contextual factors that may strengthen or weaken the position of PMs. Finally, we provide an outline of the ensuing case studies selected from different CEE countries.

The position of prime ministers in party governments

PMs occupy a central position in parliamentary democracies. As heads of government, they have the overall task of any chief executive: running the state affairs. In more concrete terms, they ought to manage a cabinet of ministers, provide stimulus and direction for domestic policies, react to unexpected events and secure the country's interests at the international stage (Strangio, 't Hart, and Walter 2013a, 1–2). For this purpose, they usually have important constitutional powers and command extensive administrative capacities which put them in a publicly visible and politically strong position (Weller 2014).

However, the actual strength of PMs may considerably differ. This is not only because prime-ministerial powers may vary from constitution to constitution but also because PMs critically depend on other political actors to remain in office and perform their tasks. Unlike chief executives in presidential systems who are popularly elected for a constitutionally fixed term, PMs head *parliamentary governments*. This means that they can be ousted by a vote of no confidence at any time and thus need to achieve and maintain the support of the parliamentary majority to stay in office. Furthermore, parliamentary systems normally have dual executives with separate heads of state (presidents or constitutional monarchs). Since especially directly elected presidents may have significant constitutional powers, they can challenge the position of PMs and tip the balance of intra-executive relations to their advantage.

At the same time, political executives in parliamentary democracies are usually *party governments*, in which policy decisions are taken by elected office-holders who are recruited and held accountable by political parties in accordance with their electoral manifesto (Katz

1987; Mair 2008, 224). The partisan organization of government has several implications for PMs to maintain their position. First, they are usually member of or closely affiliated to a party that brings them into office (Weller 1985; Helms 2002). Second, as single-party majorities in parliamentary democracies are the exception rather than the rule (Bergman, Bäck, and Hellström 2021; Bergman, Ilonszki, and Müller 2019), governments headed by PMs require the backing of other parliamentary parties, be it in the form of permanent majority coalitions or opposition parties that occasionally support minority cabinets. Third, most state presidents in parliamentary systems are also affiliated to a party because they are chosen either by parliamentary parties or in general elections whose campaigns are dominated by parties. If party affiliations of PMs and presidents do not concur, political conflicts may emerge between them, which considerably affect the PM's room for maneuver (Elgie 2008; Protsyk 2006). This might even happen if the president has to suspend her party membership after taking up office and thus becomes formally independent. Taken together, the actual strength of PMs to maintain their office results from their interrelationships with other actors in three political arenas: they have to secure the support of their *own party* as well as of a sufficient number of *other parliamentary parties* and prevail in possible conflicts with the *state president*.

Consequently, the survival in prime-ministerial office until the regular end of the parliamentary term can by no means be taken for granted but is a political achievement in its own right. Therefore, several comparative studies use the office duration of PMs as a proxy for their political "impact" (Müller and Philipp 1991, 137), "strength" or "effectiveness" (Baylis 2007, 83–84). It goes without saying that the longevity of PMs is not the most comprehensive and nuanced measure for their political strength. Indeed, a more recent approach to capture "prime-ministerial performance" refers to the main tasks of the chief executive in a parliamentary democracy and measures their successful fulfilment via a standardized expert survey (Grotz et al. 2021). Nevertheless, office duration remains a straightforward indicator that allows for a basic distinction between generally stronger and generally weaker PMs. Furthermore, it may be easily applied in both quantitative and qualitative studies to explore how they execute their office. Therefore, this book focuses on the office duration of PMs to investigate their power relationships with other political actors in the post-communist democracies of CEE.

The degree to which PMs may secure their survival in office depends on a variety of factors. Most basically, one may distinguish between two groups of explanatory variables (Dowding 2013). On the one hand, the strength of a PM depends on the availability of *individual resources* that she brings to the office (Helms 2020; Müller-Rommel, Kroeber, and Vercesi 2020). In particular, this encompasses personality traits of PMs that shape their leadership style and their ability to prevail in critical situations (Kaarbo 1997). Furthermore, their social background and their previous experience in other political career positions may equip PMs with the necessary knowledge and leadership skills, which help them to maintain their office until the regular end of the term (De Winter 1991; Müller-Rommel, Vercesi, and Berz 2022).

On the other hand, the position of a PM is significantly affected by the environment in which she operates. These *contextual features* include three different dimensions. The first dimension refers to the distribution of institutional powers that shape the PM's room for maneuver vis-à-vis the cabinet members, the parliament and the state president to different degrees and thus help her to stay in office (Bergman et al. 2003, 113). For instance, the PM can have specific prerogatives in the appointment and dismissal of cabinet members and in cabinet decision-making. Moreover, her position can be stabilized by a constructive vote of no confidence that requires the parliament to elect a successor at the same time when deposing the incumbent (Bergman et al. 2003, 180). The PM is even more institutionally strengthened, if the head of state is not directly elected and has no substantial competencies in legislative and executive matters nor any political discretion in cabinet formation and termination.

The second contextual dimension encompasses the constellation of political actors that makes it more or less difficult for a PM to stay in office. In particular, the partisan composition of a cabinet affects not only its overall stability (Grofman and van Roozendaal 1997, 424) but also the PM's position. For instance, a small number of government parties tends to lower the "internal decision-making costs of a cabinet" the PM has to lead (Helms 2005, 14). Likewise, PMs heading a majority cabinet are "generally better placed" than those heading a minority cabinet (Elgie 1995, 20). Furthermore, the partisanship of state presidents may also have considerable influence on the PM's position as the head of government, depending on whether she is a member of a cabinet party or not (Elgie 2010, 29). Finally, the parliamentary party system forms a more or less complex environment for the PM to maintain her position. In particular, if the parliament is highly fragmented or if new parties with large seat shares enter the stage, inter-party relationships become less predictable (Mainwaring, Gervasoni, and España-Najera 2017), which may hinder the PM to secure the constant support of the parliamentary majority.

Third, the socioeconomic context has general influence on the PM's room for manoeuvre. For instance, economic downturns may not only intensify partisan conflicts and lead to early cabinet dissolution (Walther and Hellström 2022, 599; Saalfeld 2013) but also force the PM to pursue radical reforms that run counter to her policy agenda and meet with fierce resistance in parliament and society, which may eventually force her to leave office prematurely (Baylis 2007, 92).

These and many other individual and contextual factors obviously affect the political survival of PMs in party governments. But which of them are most relevant in the post-communist democracies of CEE – and how do they interact in concrete cases? To receive first answers to these largely unexplored questions, we have a look at the ten PMs who had the longest tenures across the eleven CEE democracies between 1990 and 2019 (Table 1). Following the argument on the extraordinary difficulty of the post-communist context for prime-ministerial survival (Baylis 2007), we might assume that these cases have some features in common, which would suggest their particular relevance for all PMs in the region. However, what becomes immediately obvious is that the ten longest-serving heads of government in CEE operated under very different conditions. To begin with, they are distributed across seven countries. The sample includes three PMs from Slovakia and two from Slovenia while the Czech Republic, Latvia, Lithuania and Romania are not represented. However, Vacláv Klaus (Czech Republic), Algirdas Brazauskas and Andrius Kubilius (both Lithuania) served in prime-ministerial office almost as long as Janez Janša (Slovenia). Hence, we cannot easily distinguish between "favourable" and "non-favourable" country contexts for prime-ministerial survival. Furthermore, the tenure of the ten PMs was spread over the entire time period since 1990. For instance, Janez Drnovšek and Vladimír Mečiar were in power immediately after the transition to democracy, Andrius Ansip and Donald Tusk served as PMs during the 2008 economic crisis and were even reelected while Viktor Orbán and Boyko Borissov were still in office at the end of 2019.

Furthermore, Table 1 shows that the 30 cabinets led by the ten PMs vary considerably in terms of party composition. They range from single-party minority governments (Borissov I and Sanader II) to four-party surplus coalitions (Drnovšek II and Dzurinda I). Only the second cabinet of Robert Fico conforms to the conventional expectation that long-serving PMs typically head single-party majority governments. Besides, only a relative majority of these cabinets (53.3%) are minimal-winning coalitions that are generally considered to be more durable than surplus coalitions and minority government. Moreover, only four of these minimal-winning coalitions are composed of two parties (Ansip IV, Tusk I and II, Mečiar I), while the others include between three to five parties. Such high numbers of coalition parties are considered a liability for cabinet stability from a theoretical perspective. Last but not least, there are notable differences between the cabinets of one and the same PM. Merely four of the ten PMs completed their entire tenure by heading consecutive cabinets (Ansip, Dzurinda, Tusk and Sanader). The others were either forced to resign prematurely (Drnovšek, Mečiar and Borissov) or were ousted after general elections (Orban, Fico and Janša), before returning after a period in opposition.

In sum, long-serving PMs in the CEE democracies appeared across different and often difficult political contexts. This points to the general relevance not only of the PMs'

Table 1. Longest-serving PMs in 11 CEE countries (1990–2019)

PM	Country	Date in	Date out	PM duration[1]	Cabinet duration[1]	Number of cabinet parties	Cabinet type[2]
Viktor Orbán	Hungary	6 Jul 1998	21 Apr 2002	4222	1385	3	SUR
		29 May 2010	6 Apr 2014		1408	2	SUR
		10 May 2014	8 Apr 2018		1429	2	SUR
Robert Fico	Slovakia	4 Jul 2006	12 Jun 2010	3577	1439	3	MWC
		4 Apr 2012	6 Mar 2016		1432	1	SPM
		23 Mar 2016	16 Aug 2016		146	4	MWC
		1 Sep 2016	15 Mar 2018		560	3	MIN
Janez Drnovšek	Slovenia	14 May 1992	6 Dec 1992	3459	206	5	MIN
		25 Jan 1993	29 Mar 1994		428	4	SUR
		29 Mar 1994	31 Jan 1996		673	3	MWC
		31 Jan 1996	10 Nov 1996		284	2	MIN
		27 Feb 1997	8 Apr 2000		1136	3	MWC
		30 Nov 2000	2 Dec 2002		732	3	MWC
Andrus Ansip	Estonia	13 Apr 2005	4 Mar 2007	3193	690	3	MWC
		5 Apr 2007	21 May 2009		777	3	MWC
		4 Jun 2009	6 Mar 2011		640	2	MIN
		5 Apr 2011	26 Mar 2014		1086	2	MWC
Mikuláš Dzurinda	Slovakia	30 Oct 1998	21 Sep 2002	2633	1422	4	SUR
		16 Oct 2002	8 Feb 2006		1211	4	MWC
Donald Tusk	Poland	16 Nov 2007	9 Oct 2011	2462	1423	2	MWC
		18 Nov 2011	22 Sep 2014		1039	2	MWC
Vladimír Mečiar	Slovakia	24 Jun 1992	15 Mar 1994	2046	629	2	MWC
		13 Dec 1994	30 Oct 1998		1417	3	MWC
Boyko Borissov	Bulgaria	27 Jul 2009	21 Feb 2013	2045	1305	1	MIN
		7 Nov 2014	16 Nov 2016		740	3	MIN
Ivo Sanader	Croatia	23 Dec 2003	9 Feb 2006	2022	779	2	MIN
		9 Feb 2006	12 Jan 2008		702	1	MIN
		12 Jan 2008	6 Jul 2009		541	4	MWC
Janez Janša	Slovenia	3 Dec 2004	21 Sep 2008	1805	1388	4	MWC
		28 Jan 2012	20 Mar 2013		417	5	MWC

Notes: The countries included are Bulgaria, Croatia, Czech Republic, Estonia, Latvia, Lithuania, Hungary, Poland, Romania, Slovakia and Slovenia. The timeframe under consideration is between the first parliamentary elections after state independence (from 2000 in Croatia) up to the end of 2019. Only completed cabinets are included (PMs Orbán and Borissov were in office beyond the end of 2019).
[1]Office duration in days.
[2]MIN-minority; MWC-minimal winning coalition; SPM-single-party majority; SUR-surplus.

individual characteristics but also of the interplay between these characteristics and contextual factors that strengthened or weakened their position in chief executive office (Elgie 2018). Given the multitude of contextual factors and the scarce literature on PMs in post-communist democracies, this article does not aim to examine the influence of a battery of variables on prime-ministerial survival in a cross-national perspective. Rather, we will subsequently elaborate on the interrelationships of the PMs with their own party, other parliamentary parties and state presidents in the CEE democracies. In doing so, we will explore some specific features cross-nationally and over time, which are particularly relevant to understand the position of PMs in these three arenas. These findings also guide the selection of the case studies, which trace the mechanisms of prime-ministerial survival in the following contributions to this volume.

Prime ministers and their parties

In modern parliamentary democracies, political parties seek to monopolize the access to prime-ministerial office, which enables them to dominate the domestic policy agenda and gain visibility and popularity among voters. Hence, they are keen to appoint one of their own members as PM. Once this is achieved, parties need to ensure that the PM enacts their preferred policies and upholds their profile among the voters. For that purpose, they have developed various control mechanisms, including the removal of the PM as the last resort (Samuels and Shugart 2010). However, given the benefits that parties receive from occupying PM office, they have a vital interest in backing their PMs, which rather stabilizes the latter in office. Therefore, the interrelationship between PMs and their own parties, and consequently prime-ministerial survival, may significantly depend on whether PM is a party leader or not. In general, when PMs are also party leaders, this brings distinct advantages to both sides: visibility for parties and political support for PMs.

There are good reasons for parties to nominate their leaders as PM. Before becoming party leader, a politician has to undergo a rigorous pre-screening within the party and gain acceptance of its most powerful members and bodies by demonstrating her adherence to the party's policy line. Furthermore, PM parties prefer to nominate a candidate whom voters can most clearly associate with them. As the most recognizable party member, their leader is an appropriate choice (Grotz and Weber 2017, 230). Party leaders are also more likely to pursue nomination as PM, as they know that their parties have strong incentives to assist them in this office. Therefore, we expect that PMs in CEE tend to be party leaders.

At the same time, PMs who are party leaders may fulfil the chief executive tasks more successfully (Grotz et al. 2021) and survive longer in office (Grotz and Weber 2017). As the electoral appeal of the PM party largely depends on government success, it usually has a great interest to hold its leader in the chief executive position. Moreover, it is easier for a party-leader PM to actively organize parliamentary support for government policy. To do so, party leaders need to maintain the policy profile of the party, aided by extensive institutional and informal prerogatives to ensure the backing of the party's legislative wing (Carey 2007, 93; Müller 2000, 316).

These expectations are clearly confirmed by a survey of all PMs in eleven CEE democracies from 1990 to 2019 (Table 2). Overall, more than a half of the PMs were party leaders before their accession to chief executive office (55.1%). The significance of being a party leader is further underlined by the fact that several PMs assumed this office after becoming PMs (13.4%). At the same time, there is considerable variation between the CEE countries. The general pattern is clearly observable in Croatia, Czech Republic, Slovakia and

Slovenia, where nearly all PMs were party leaders. This stands in contrast to Romania, Latvia and Poland with a majority of non-party leader PMs. More generally, the selection of party leaders as PMs in CEE significantly depends on the timing of government formation. Following Grotz and Weber (2017), the above-mentioned advantages for parties to have their leader in prime-ministerial office are confined to "post-electoral contexts". When the complete parliamentary term is still ahead, a PM is expected to have enough time to fulfil the chief executive tasks successfully so that her party may particularly profit from her leadership performance at the next polls because she is the party's main face. Therefore,

> even if the leader of this party is not at the disposal for premiership and another person takes over the position, the party may offer the latter its chairmanship in order to gain from his or her public visibility as PM and to reap the benefits of a likely stable government.
>
> (Grotz and Weber 2017, 235)

Table 2. PM duration by party leadership in CEE democracies (1990–2019)

Country	Number of PMs by party leadership status				PM office duration			
	Party leader before[1]	Party leader during[2]	Not party leader[3]	Total	Party leader before[1]	Party leader during[2]	Not party leader[3]	Total
Bulgaria	6 (66.7)	1 (11.1)	2 (22.2)	9	1023	1305	516	942
Croatia	6 (85.7)	0 (0.0)	1 (14.3)	7	1002	-	146	879
Czech Republic	8 (88.9)	1 (11.1)	0 (0.0)	9	940	404	-	881
Estonia	9 (69.2)	3 (23.1)	1 (7.7)	13	825	589	122	717
Hungary	5 (50.0)	1 (10.0)	4 (40.0)	10	1386	1038	481	989
Latvia	5 (27.8)	3 (16.7)	10 (55.5)	18	356	634	502	483
Lithuania	5 (41.7)	2 (16.6)	5 (41.7)	12	986	954	516	785
Poland	5 (33.3)	2 (13.3)	8 (53.4)	15	850	911	445	642
Romania	5 (35.7)	1 (7.1)	8 (57.2)	14	1023	-	439	662
Slovakia	7 (77.8)	1 (11.1)	1 (11.1)	9	1179	272	459	999
Slovenia	9 (81.8)	2 (18.2)	0 (0.0)	11	901	392	-	809
Total	70 (55.1)	17 (13.4)	40 (31.5)	127	950	697	459	761

Source: Authors' compilation based on various internet sources.
Notes: A PM term ends when (1) PM is replaced or (2) new elections occur. The data include PMs since the first parliamentary elections after state independence (from 2000 in Croatia) up to the end of 2019. Only completed cabinets are included. Caretaker cabinets are excluded. Percentages are indicated in parentheses. Average office durations are given in days.
[1] The category includes PMs who were party leaders before assuming PM office.
[2] The category includes PMs who attained party leadership during their PM office.
[3] The category includes PM who never held party leadership position.

By contrast, if a PM has to be installed in the middle or even towards the end of the parliamentary term, the time for the new incumbent to perform successfully might be too short, and her tenure could be overshadowed by the failure of the preceding cabinet, if some of the old government parties also take part in the new cabinet. In such "replacement contexts", the PM party tends to suffer from the weaker performance of the new head of government in the upcoming elections. Therefore, it might keep its leader out of the line of fire and rather select a person with previous cabinet experience who performs the prime-ministerial tasks in the best possible way during the remaining term. This pattern is particularly pronounced in Romania, where "technocrats" took over the premiership in replacement contexts especially if there was few time left to the next elections (Ştefan 2020). Furthermore, several party leaders in CEE decided against taking up the PM office for strategic reasons. In Poland, for instance, the Chairman of the Solidarity Electoral Action (AWS), Marian Krzaklewski, sought to stand in the 2000 presidential elections and therefore did not take over the premiership because he wanted to "avoid a fall in approval ratings" if leading an internally heterogeneous party government (Zuba 2020, 52). Likewise, Jarosław Kaczyński, leader of the Law and Justice Party (PiS), shied away from becoming PM after the 2005 parliamentary elections because he did not want to jeopardize the chances of his twin brother in the upcoming presidential race (Grotz and Weber 2017, 244).

Table 2 also reveals that party-leader PMs in CEE have overall been longer in office than their counterparts who were not party leaders. Even those PMs who became party leaders after assuming chief executive office have a substantially longer tenure than non-party leaders. This pattern not only is most pronounced in Hungary, Croatia, Slovakia and Estonia but also applies to the other CEE countries to a larger or minor extent. The only exception is Latvia, where PMs without party leadership were not only more frequent but also had longer average tenures than those who had been party leader before. This deviant case can be generally explained with the relatively high fragmentation and fluidity of the Latvian party system and the resulting cabinet instability (Ikstens and Balcere 2019). Nevertheless, even in Latvia those PMs who became party leader after resuming chief executive office had a longer average tenure than the others.

Prime ministers and other parliamentary parties

Beyond their own party, PMs also rely on other parliamentary parties that have joined their government as coalition partners. To solve severe intra-coalition conflicts and to prove executive leadership, a PM may try to fire unsuccessful ministers and hire new ones. However, this active mode of cabinet reshuffle is typical of single-party governments in Westminster democracies (Indridason and Kam 2008), while it usually meets more resistance in multi-party governments – both from the PM's party and from other coalition partners. Accordingly, the multi-party cabinets in post-communist democracies have seen much more "passive reshuffles" that may occur because of personal reasons, political scandals or intra-party struggles, rather than those proactively launched by the PM. In any case, cabinet reshuffles do not stabilize post-communist PMs in office but tend to affect their performance (Grotz, Kroeber, and Kukec 2022).

Even worse for the political survival of PMs is the break-up of the incumbent government coalition, which might also imply the end of her own tenure. While a high congruence between prime-ministerial and party-government survival seems to be plausible, there are also two alternative possibilities. On the one hand, government parties may withdraw their support in a PM and replace her without changing the partisan composition of government or calling early elections. On the other hand, a PM may reorganize the partisan composition of her government and thus succeed to survive in office. For instance, she might replace an outgoing party with another one to preserve the parliamentary majority or simply continue by leading a minority government if the departure of a party entails losing the majority status. These distinct scenarios allow for a more nuanced understanding of the relationship between PMs and their government parties. The success of a PM to outlive her party government demonstrates her ability to maintain office even in critical circumstances. By contrast, the continuity of a party government rather points to the notable weakness of the outgoing PM, who lost the backing not only from other parliamentary parties but also from her own party.

The general expectation of congruent durations of PMs and their party governments in CEE is overall confirmed. As Table 3 shows, there have been only slightly more party governments than PMs, and accordingly, the PMs have tended to stay in office a little longer than the partisan composition of their cabinets. However, the country-level analysis reveals considerable variation. In Bulgaria, Lithuania and Slovakia the relative duration of PMs and party governments broadly conform to the congruity observed at the CEE level. By contrast, party governments in the Czech Republic and Hungary are more durable than the respective PMs. In the Czech Republic this was mainly due to the 2002–2006 parliamentary term when three different PMs from the Social democrats (ČSSD) – Vladimír Špidla, Stanislav Gross and Jiří Paroubek – were consecutively in power while the government coalition of the ČSSD with the Christian democrats (KDU-ČSL) and the liberal US-DEU endured until regular elections. Similarly, Hungary saw two turnovers of Socialist

Table 3. Duration of PMs, party governments and cabinets in CEE democracies (1990–2019)

Country	Prime ministers		Party governments		Cabinets	
	N	Duration	N	Duration	N	Duration
Bulgaria	9	941	8	983	9	941
Croatia	7	879	10	616	11	560
Czech Republic	9	880	8	991	10	792
Estonia	13	717	15	622	16	583
Hungary	10	989	8	1236	11	899
Latvia	18	483	21	413	23	377
Lithuania	12	785	12	785	15	628
Poland	15	642	13	741	18	535
Romania	14	662	18	500	24	386
Slovakia	9	999	9	936	10	899
Slovenia	11	809	15	593	15	593
Total	127	761	137	695	162	597

Sources: see Table 2.

Notes: A PM term ends when the PM is replaced or new elections occur. A party government is terminated when the party composition of cabinet changes or new elections occur. Cabinet ends with PM replacement, change of party composition or new elections. The data include PMs since the first parliamentary elections after state independence (from 2000 in Croatia) up to the end of 2019. Only completed cabinets are included. Caretaker cabinets are excluded. Average office durations are given in days.

PMs – from Péter Medgyessy to Ferenc Gyurcsány in 2004 and from Gyurcsány to Gordon Bajnai in 2009 – without affecting the government's party composition. Furthermore, Hungary's first post-communist PM, József Antall, was replaced after his death in 1993 by Péter Boross who completed the parliamentary term with the conservative three-party government. In the remaining CEE countries, the average tenure of PMs was longer than the duration of their respective party governments. This particularly applies to Croatia and Slovenia where PMs like Janez Drnovšek or Ivo Sanader displayed outstanding ability to remain in office by reorganizing the party composition of their cabinets. Again, Latvia stands out with the highest number of PMs and an even higher number of party governments, which had the least average durations among all other CEE countries.

While these distinct patterns of prime-ministerial tenure and party-government duration are clearly visible in CEE, the extant literature has not elaborated on the conditions under which they occur. As a first step towards such an understanding, we explore selected factors that might critically affect the stability of both PMs and party governments in post-communist democracies. In general, the standard attributes for explaining cabinet stability (Müller, Bergman, and Strøm 2008, 20–23; Grofman and van Roozendaal 1997) may also be suitable for exploring the political survival of PMs. In the following, we concentrate on two attributes of party governments that may be considered particularly relevant in the CEE context.

The first attribute undermining the stability of party governments is their *minority status*. Minority governments entail continuous bargaining with opposition parties, spearheaded by PMs as their heads. Therefore, the minority status of a cabinet highlights the relevance of the wider parliamentary constellation beyond government parties. In particular, extremist parties usually refuse to enter government or are permanently excluded from the coalition formation process since they stand in fundamental opposition to parliamentary democracy and seek to bring down any party government. Thus, strong extremist parties in parliament may critically affect the survival of minority cabinets and of their PMs (Warwick 1994, 63). Other opposition parties may be willing to cooperate with the government to varying degrees, by entering rather stable agreements with minority governments or supporting them on an ad-hoc basis. The lack of credible commitment by opposition parties may motivate these parties to negotiate alternative coalitions, thus frustrating the policy agenda of PMs and possibly ousting them from office (Somer-Topcu and Williams 2008, 317).

Second, the involvement of *genuinely new parties* (GNPs) in governments has largely escaped the attention of Western literature on coalition governance, but there are good reasons to assume that GNPs may negatively influence the stability of both PMs and party governments in CEE. By definition, new parties have no governing experience and often lack a clear ideological profile, which makes coalition negotiations more unpredictable and prone to failure (Grotz and Weber 2016, 452). Nevertheless, GNPs are a recurring feature of CEE party systems and frequently participate in governments of the region (Tavits 2008, 114).

Table 4 shows that 102 of the 162 prime-ministerial cabinets in our sample were backed by a parliamentary majority, while only 60 had a minority status. Most minority cabinets were found in Romania (14), Latvia (9) and Croatia (6), while they remained quite exceptional in Hungary (2) and Slovakia (3). As expected, minority cabinets had a significantly lower duration than majority cabinets, both overall and in the individual countries. The only exception is Romania where the minority cabinets on average

Table 4. Cabinet duration by cabinet type and inclusion of GNPs in CEE cabinets (1990–2019)

	Majority cabinet (N/duration)	Minority cabinet (N/duration)	GNP in cabinet (N/duration)	No GNP in cabinet (N/duration)	PM from GNP (N/duration)	PM not from GNP (N/duration)	Total (N/duration)
Bulgaria	4 (1261)	5 (686)	3 (1159)	6 (833)	2 (1369)	7 (819)	9 (941)
Croatia	5 (663)	6 (473)	2 (168)	9 (647)	0 (-)	11 (560)	11 (560)
Czech Republic	6 (854)	4 (700)	2 (1246)	8 (679)	0 (-)	10 (792)	10 (792)
Estonia	12 (622)	4 (466)	2 (457)	14 (601)	1 (714)	15 (575)	16 (583)
Hungary	9 (1019)	2 (362)	0 (-)	11 (899)	0 (-)	11 (899)	11 (899)
Latvia	14 (436)	9 (285)	13 (364)	10 (395)	6 (273)	17 (414)	23 (377)
Lithuania	10 (646)	5 (592)	4 (539)	11 (660)	0 (-)	15 (628)	15 (628)
Poland	14 (599)	4 (313)	0 (-)	18 (535)	0 (-)	18 (535)	18 (535)
Romania	10 (335)	14 (423)	1 (903)	23 (364)	0 (-)	24 (386)	24 (386)
Slovakia	7 (1099)	3 (430)	3 (1031)	7 (842)	0 (-)	10 (899)	10 (899)
Slovenia	11 (738)	4 (195)	3 (731)	12 (558)	2 (889)	13 (547)	15 (593)
Total	102 (689)	60 (441)	33 (615)	129 (592)	11 (624)	151 (595)	162 (597)

Source: Authors' compilation based on various internet sources.

Notes: A cabinet ends when (1) PM is replaced, (2) new elections occur or (3) cabinet party composition changes. The data include PMs since the first parliamentary elections after state independence (from 2000 in Croatia) up to the end of 2019. Only completed cabinets are included. Caretaker cabinets are excluded. Average office durations are given in days.

lasted a bit longer than majority cabinets. Yet, cabinet stability in Romania was at a very low level compared to all other CEE countries except for Latvia. Of course, one has to bear in mind that many minority cabinets were formed during the parliamentary term and thus did not have as much time left as those majority cabinets that came into office immediately after elections. But even if we focus only on cabinets formed in the post-electoral context, the duration of minority cabinets is considerably shorter (20 cabinets with the average duration of 523 days) than that of majority cabinets (59 cabinets with the average duration of 878 days). Moreover, there were some minority cabinets formed during the parliamentary term that broke apart before its regular end. Overall, these patterns suggest that minority cabinets have been a liability for post-communist PMs to survive in office.

Merely a fifth (20.4%) of the cabinets in our sample included one or more genuinely new parties, and these were unevenly distributed among the CEE countries. Almost 40% of the cabinets with GNPs were found in Latvia, whereas Poland and Hungary have not seen any GNP in their post-communist governments. Nevertheless, aggregate duration of cabinets with GNPs has been slightly longer than that of cabinets composed of established parties only. To make sense of this rather unexpected finding, a closer look reveals that the overall longer duration of cabinets with GNPs is present in five CEE countries only (Bulgaria, Czech Republic, Romania, Slovakia and Slovenia). Among the relevant cabinets, those stand out that were led by a PM coming from a genuinely new party. Apart from the quite specific context of Latvia, these PMs were rather few but significantly longer in office than their national counterparts (Table 4). These cases include the former tsar Saxecoburggotski (National Movement Simeon the Second) and Boyko Borissov (GERB) in Bulgaria, Juhan Parts (Res Publica) in Estonia and Alenka Bratušek (Positive Slovenia) and Miro Cerar (Party of Miro Cerar) in Slovenia. Apart from Bratušek, all of them played the lead in the foundation of their party and took over the chief executive after a landslide electoral victory, which provided them favourable starting conditions to remain in office for long time.

Hence, it seems to matter for prime-ministerial survival if the GNP nominates the PM or joins the cabinet as a junior partner because in the latter case it may challenge the position of a PM from an established party. This is underlined by a closer inspection of the two Czech cabinets that included GNPs and had the longest duration among all cases in this category. After the 2010 elections, ODS chairman Petr Nečas formed a majority coalition with the party TOP09 and the new Public Affairs party (VV). He could remain in prime-ministerial office for quite some time but eventually lost the support of the parliamentary majority because the VV group broke apart. In the end, he was ousted by a vote of no confidence in June 2013 (Linek 2014). Similarly, ČSSD leader Bohuslav Sobotka included the new ANO party founded by the tycoon Andrej Babiš into his three-party majority government after the 2013 election. Although this cabinet stayed in office until the regular parliamentary term, constant conflicts with Babiš compromised Sobotka's performance as PM and left him politically damaged so that he renounced his candidacy for the 2017 elections that were won by ANO (Petrúšek and Kudrnáč 2017). Overall, these case illustrations highlight the need to go beyond the formal duration when exploring the mechanisms between the presence of GNPs in cabinet and the political survival of PMs.

Prime ministers and state presidents

Parliamentary democracies are characterized by dual executives, and in CEE in particular, PMs coexist with presidents, which are considerably involved in politics (Protsyk 2006). Besides the popular mandate and the significant powers that most heads of state in the region enjoy, highly volatile party systems and frequent government crises gave the impression of presidents as the beacons of political stability in the post-communist context. At the same time, the weakness of PMs in CEE may be partially attributed to powerful presidents, who staged serious conflicts with PMs and even forced some of them out of office (Baylis 2007, 89).

The extent to which presidents are likely to mount a challenge on the PMs depends on their constitutional powers (Bucur and Cheibub 2017; Schleiter and Morgan-Jones 2009). Besides commanding a popular mandate, some presidents are granted considerable competencies. To capture these presidential powers, many studies follow the seminal approach by Shugart and Carey (1992). They distinguish between presidential prerogatives in the legislative process (legislative powers) and those regarding the composition of the cabinet and the survival of the assembly (non-legislative powers) that are summed up to an overall index of presidential power (Shugart and Carey 1992). Based on such institutional equipment, presidents may impose their own political agenda upon the government.

Presidents are especially motivated to interfere in the work of PMs when they are affiliated to an opposition party. In many democracies, it has become common practice that presidential candidates are party members or at least receive campaign assistance from parties, which compels them to act in partisan manner once they win the presidency (Savage 2018). The occurrence of a "cohabitation" between presidents and PMs, where the president is affiliated to a party not included in the cabinet (Elgie 2010, 29), may undermine the legislative agenda of the acting party government and its political survival.

On the other hand, when the president is affiliated to the PM party or another party of the government coalition, PMs may count on the support of an important ally. Therefore, political conflicts between PMs and presidents under cohabitation might be reflected in a shorter office duration of PMs compared to cases in which the intra-executive partisan constellation is congruent. Since powerful "hostile" presidents may seriously affect the position of PM, we expect that cohabitation shortens prime-ministerial duration particularly when presidents command substantial constitutional powers.

Table 5 shows the patterns of presidential powers and their partisan congruence with PMs in the eleven CEE democracies, as well as the average prime-ministerial duration under the different constellations. To begin with, the constitutional powers of state presidents are measured by a composite index including their legislative and non-legislative competencies following Shugart and Carey's approach (Bairett 2015; Andrews and Bairett 2019). Accordingly, Poland and Romania have the most powerful presidents, while the weakest ones are found in the Czech Republic, Latvia and Slovenia. Among the two sub-dimensions of presidential powers, the non-legislative powers deserve particular attention in the present context because they include the presidential prerogatives in cabinet formation and dismissal, which might have a more immediate and stronger impact on prime-ministerial survival than presidential veto powers in the legislative process. In this regard, it is remarkable to note that some of the overall weaker presidents in CEE possess significant powers. This is especially true not only for the Lithuanian president but also for the Slovenian one, which has no relevant legislative powers at all but considerable discretion in the processes of cabinet formation and dismissal.

Table 5. PM duration by PM-president partisanship congruence in CEE democracies (1990–2019)

Country	Presidential powers		PMs by PM-president partisanship congruence			PM duration by partisanship congruence			
	Direct election[1]	Power index[2]	Congruent[3]	Cohabitation	Independent	Congruent[3]	Cohabitation	Independent	Total
Poland	Y	13 (6/7)	9 (60.0)	6 (40.0)	0 (0.0)	616	683	-	642
Romania	Y	13 (7/6)	8 (57.2)	5 (35.7)	1 (7.1)	834	442	391	662
Hungary	N	11 (6/5)	3 (30.0)	3 (30.0)	4 (40.0)	1415	948	700	989
Croatia	Y	11 (6/5)	5 (57.1)	3 (42.9)	0 (0.0)	813	968	-	879
Lithuania	Y	11 (4/7)	2 (16.7)	0 (0.0)	10 (83.3)	663	-	809	785
Slovakia	Y	9 (3/6)	3 (33.3)	5 (55.6)	1 (11.1)	1156	963	706	999
Estonia	N	9 (5/4)	7 (53.9)	6 (46.1)	0 (0.0)	653	792	-	717
Bulgaria	Y	8 (3/5)	4 (44.4)	4 (44.4)	1 (11.1)	1001	965	611	942
Czech Republic	N	6 (2/4)	2 (22.2)	4 (44.5)	3 (33.3)	974	698	1062	881
Latvia	N	6 (4/2)	6 (33.3)	3 (16.7)	9 (50.0)	508	476	469	483
Slovenia	Y	5 (0/5)	3 (27.3)	1 (9.1)	7 (63.6)	810	1388	725	809
Total	-	8.5	51 (40.2)	40 (31.5)	36 (28.3)	794	777	697	761

Sources: see Table 2.

Notes: A PM term ends when (1) PM is replaced or (2) new elections occur. The data include PMs since the first parliamentary elections after state independence (from 2000 in Croatia) up to the end of 2019. Only completed cabinets are included. Caretaker cabinets are excluded. Percentages are indicated in parentheses. Average office durations are given in days.

[1] In the Czech Republic and Slovakia, the state president was elected by parliament until 2009 and 1999, respectively.

[2] The index is the sum of scores for legislative and non-legislative presidential powers (values for sub-dimensions in parentheses; Andrews and Bairett 2019).

[3] The partisanship of PM and president is congruent if president is (was until elected) a member of PM party or other coalition party. Independent means that the president has no formal party affiliation.

These general patterns of presidential powers in post-communist democracies are not systematically linked to prime-ministerial duration. Polish and Romanian PMs have relatively short office durations, which may be traced back to the substantial presidential powers in these countries. However, Latvian PMs held office for an average of only 483 days, despite constitutionally weak presidents. Other outliers are the PMs in Hungary, Croatia and Slovakia who recorded an above-average longevity while serving alongside considerably powerful presidents.

Turning to the patterns of partisan congruence, a plurality of PMs (40.2%) served under presidents from the same party or another government party, while almost a third experienced a cohabitation. There is also a considerable number of PMs who governed under independent presidents. Interestingly, the frequency of independent presidents seems not to be systematically related to their election mode, as relevant cases have frequently appeared not only in Lithuania and Slovenia (direct elections) but also in Latvia and Hungary (indirect elections). At large, PMs in CEE tend to be shorter in office under cohabitation than under congruent intra-executive constellations in most countries. However, this overall difference is not as pronounced as expected, and there are remarkable exceptions, most prominently in Slovenia, where the average tenure of PMs was much longer under cohabitation than in the other constellations. Even more remarkably, prime-ministerial duration is the shortest when presidents are not affiliated to any party, which does not fit the conventional wisdom about partisan presidents and their relations with PMs.

At the country level, there seems to be more variation between the three categories. This heterogeneity might be due to different degrees of presidential powers, as opposition-affiliated presidents are more likely to undermine the survival of PMs the more powerful they are. Among the six countries with the most powerful presidents, three have a significantly higher office duration of PMs who did not serve under presidents from opposition parties (Romania, Hungary and Slovakia), which partially corroborates the theoretical expectation. In Poland, however, the difference in PM duration between congruent and non-congruent constellation is quite small although the country has the most powerful presidency in the region. Another exceptional case is Lithuania, where independent presidents seem to be more favourable for PM survival than presidents affiliated to government parties. Croatian PMs under cohabitation also have a small advantage over those in congruent constellation. This might be partially attributed to the exclusion of the Plenković II cabinet from the dataset (ended in May 2020), which lasted for nearly the complete legislative term in parallel to president Grabar-Kitarović who was supported by HDZ.

Outline of the volume

While PMs enjoy substantial powers to accomplish their diverse tasks, their political survival depends on various conditions within three arenas: their relationship with their own parties, with other parliamentary parties and with state presidents. Exploring the overall patterns of prime-ministerial duration in CEE, this article attempted to provide a systematic overview of these conditions. The relationship between PMs and their own parties is more stable when PMs are party leaders. This has been the case for nearly two-thirds of PMs in CEE since 1990, and these PMs were considerably longer in office than other PMs. Moreover, some PMs managed to outlive their original party governments, whereas others were replaced and their party governments continued. While minority cabinets provide an obvious challenge for post-communist PMs to remain in office, the impact of genuinely new government parties on their survival is less straightforward. Finally, the position of PMs in CEE is dependent on the partisan congruence between presidents and parliamentary majorities, particularly if the former command considerable constitutional powers. Arguably, the way these conditions affect the tenure of individual PMs separately and interactively seems peculiar to contextual circumstances. This invites for in-depth studies of deliberately selected cases, like those included in this book.

The first article by Dario Nikić Čakar and Alenka Krašovec explores the survival strategies of PMs, when GNPs participate in government. Croatia and Slovenia offer particularly fruitful cases for this purpose. In both countries, GNPs have succeeded to win large vote shares and to enter parliament during the last decade. Moreover, they occasionally played a pivotal role in government formation. In Croatia, The Bridge of Independent Lists (Most) joined the cabinets led by Tihomir Orešković (2016) and Andrej Plenković (2016/2017) as a junior partner. Slovenia has seen even more GNPs entering parliament and government, including the List of Zoran Janković–Positive Slovenia (LZJ-PS) and the Party of Miro Cerar (SMC) that received the largest seat shares in the 2011 and 2014 parliamentary elections. However, while Cerar became the head of a post-electoral coalition government, Janković was prevented from taking over the chief executive position before his protégé Alenka Bratušek became the head of government in 2012. Hence, the mentioned PMs in Slovenia and Croatia had to deal with GNPs in different constellations. At the same time, their tenures varied in specific ways: while Orešković and Bratušek occupied the prime-ministerial office only for quite short periods, Plenković and Cerar survived for complete parliamentary terms. Therefore, these four cases form an interesting sample to explore prime-ministerial survival with GNPs in government.

Maria Spirova and Radostina Sharenkova-Toshkova focus on a striking case of prime-ministerial survival. In Bulgaria, Boyko Borissov came to power after the 2009 parliamentary election under most unfavourable circumstances: leader of a new party, he only maintained a minority in parliament and had to cope with an ideologically heterogeneous coalition. But although Borissov resigned from office in 2013 and 2016 when he did not have to, he returned to power and became the longest serving PM in the country. Against this background, this article investigates Borissov's three cabinets with special emphasis on his relationship with other parties inside and outside parliament, his personnel policies and his strategic use of institutional opportunities.

Thereafter, Daniel Kovarek deals with the only two minority governments in post-communist Hungary, led by Ferenc Gyurcsány and Gordon Bajnai, respectively. These single-party cabinets, supported by the Socialists (MSZP) and largely relying on liberal (SZDSZ) MPs for legislative majorities, differed considerably with regard to their policy performance. Hence, they provide an excellent opportunity for exploring prime-ministerial leadership and survival under a minority government in a majoritarian institutional setting and a polarized political context.

Lukas Pukelis and Mažvydas Jastramskis turn to another difficult constellation considered typical for post-communist party governments: the "intrusion" of directly elected state presidents into the PM's discretion. More specifically, they explore the presidential influence on cabinet composition in Lithuania. The Lithuanian context seems to be most suitable in this regard because the country has seen the constant election of independent presidents since 1998. But although there were almost no formal cohabitations during the last two decades, presidential activism in the field of ministerial selection has differed significantly. To explain this variation, the authors concentrate on the political resources of the respective PMs and their party governments.

The last case study in this volume deals with post-communist Romania that is generally known for having powerful state presidents and weak PMs. Laurenţiu Ştefan challenges this conventional assumption by exploring the conditional influence of presidents on prime-ministerial survival for all Romanian chief executives since 1989. He shows that Romanian presidents do not have constitutional powers to dismiss the head of government but can nevertheless initiate and steer the process through which a PM eventually leaves office. However, the actual power of presidents to end the PM's tenure largely depends on their political convergence with the parliamentary majority. The final contribution by Marko Kukec and Florian Grotz summarizes the main findings of the preceding articles and suggests some avenues for further research on PMs in CEE and other parliamentary democracies.

Acknowledgements

We would especially like to thank Ferdinand Müller-Rommel, the anonymous reviewer and the participants of a workshop held at the Helmut Schmidt University, Hamburg, on 18–20 September 2019 on which first drafts of the papers included in this Special Issue were discussed.

Disclosure statement

No potential conflict of interest was reported by the authors.

Funding

We gratefully acknowledge the generous funding by the German Research Foundation (DFG) (Grants GR3311/3-1 and MU618/18-1).

ORCID

Florian Grotz http://orcid.org/0000-0002-7512-2526
Marko Kukec http://orcid.org/0000-0002-9453-2977

References

Andrews, Josephine T., and Richard L. Bairett. 2019. "Measuring Executive Power." Unpublished working paper.

Bairett, Richard L. 2015. "Executive Power and Media Freedom in Central and Eastern Europe." *Comparative Political Studies* 48 (10): 1260–92.

Baylis, Thomas A. 2007. "Embattled Executives: Prime Ministerial Weakness in East Central Europe." *Communist and Post-Communist Studies* 40 (1): 81–106.

Bergman, Torbjörn, Hanna Bäck, and Johan Hellström, eds. 2021. *Coalition Governance in Western Europe*. Oxford: Oxford University Press.

Bergman, Torbjörn, Gabriella Ilonszki, and Wolfgang C. Müller, eds. 2019. *Coalition Governance in Central Eastern Europe*. Oxford: Oxford University Press.

Bergman, Torbjörn, Wolfgang C. Müller, Kaare Strøm, and Magnus Blomgren. 2003. "Democratic Delegation and Accountability: Cross-National Patterns." In *Delegation and Accountability in Parliamentary Democracies*, edited by Kaare Strøm, Wolfgang C. Müller, and Torbjörn Bergman, 109–220. Oxford: Oxford University Press.

Blondel, Jean, and Ferdinand Müller-Rommel. 2001. *Cabinets in Eastern Europe*. Edited by Jean Blondel and Ferdinand Müller-Rommel. London: Palgrave.

Blondel, Jean, Ferdinand Müller-Rommel, and Darina Malová. 2007. *Governing New European Democracies*. Basingstoke: Palgrave Macmillan.

Bucur, Cristina, and José Antonio Cheibub. 2017. "Presidential Partisanship in Government Formation: Do Presidents Favor Their Parties When They Appoint the Prime Minister?" *Political Research Quarterly* 70 (4): 803–17.

Carey, John M. 2007. "Competing Principals, Political Institutions, and Party Unity in Legislative Voting." *American Journal of Political Science* 51 (1): 92–107.

Dowding, Keith. 2013. "Prime-Ministerial Power: Institutional and Personal Factors." In *Understanding Prime-Ministerial Performance: Comparative Perspectives*, edited by Paul Strangio, Paul 't Hart, and James Walter, 57–78. Oxford: Oxford University Press.

Elgie, Robert. 1995. *Political Leadership in Liberal Democracies*. London: Macmillan Press.

———. 2008. "The Perils of Semi-Presidentialism. Are They Exaggerated?" *Democratization* 15 (1): 49–66.

———. 2010. "Semi-Presidentialism, Cohabitation and the Collapse of Electoral Democracies, 1990–2008." *Government and Opposition* 45 (1): 29–49.

———. 2018. *Political Leadership: A Pragmatic Institutionalist Approach*. London: Palgrave Macmillan.

Fettelschoss, Katja, and Csaba Nikolenyi. 2008. "Learning to Rule: Ministerial Careers in Post-Communist Democracies." In *The Selection of Ministers in Europe: Hiring and Firing*, edited by Keith Dowding and Patrick Dumont, 204–27. London: Routledge.

Grofman, Bernard, and Peter van Roozendaal. 1997. "Modelling Cabinet Durability and Termination." *British Journal of Political Science* 27 (3): 419–51.

Grotz, Florian, Corinna Kroeber, and Marko Kukec. 2022. "Cabinet Reshuffles and Prime-Ministerial Performance in Central and Eastern Europe." *Government and Opposition*, online first.

Grotz, Florian, Ferdinand Müller-Rommel, Jan Berz, Corinna Kroeber, and Marko Kukec. 2021. "How Political Careers Affect Prime-Ministerial Performance: Evidence from Central and Eastern Europe." *Comparative Political Studies* 54 (11): 1907–38.

Grotz, Florian, and Till Weber. 2012. "Party Systems and Government Stability in Central and Eastern Europe." *World Politics* 64 (4): 699–740.

———. 2016. "New Parties, Information Uncertainty, and Government Formation: Evidence from Central and Eastern Europe." *European Political Science Review* 8 (3): 449–72.

———. 2017. "Prime Ministerial Tenure in Central and Eastern Europe: The Role of Party Leadership and Cabinet Experience." In *Parties, Governments and Elites: The Comparative Study of Democracy*, edited by Philipp Harfst, Ina Kubbe, and Thomas Poguntke, 225–44. Wiesbaden: Springer.

Helms, Ludger. 2002. "'Chief Executives' and Their Parties: The Case of Germany." *German Politics* 11 (2): 146–64.

———. 2005. *Presidents, Prime Ministers and Chancellors: Executive Leadership in Western Democracies*. Basingstoke: Palgrave Macmillan.

———. 2020. "Performance and Evaluation of Political Executives." In *The Oxford Handbook of Political Executives*, edited by Rudy B. Andeweg, Robert Elgie, Ludger Helms, Juliet Kaarbo, and Ferdinand Müller-Rommel, 646–70. Oxford: Oxford University Press.

Hloušek, Vít. 2015. "Two Types of Presidentialization in the Party Politics of Central Eastern Europe." *Rivista Italiana di Scienza Politica* 45 (3): 277–99.

Ikstens, Jānis, and Ilze Balcere. 2019. "Latvia: Office-Seeking in an Ethnically Divided Polity." In *Coalition Governance in Central Eastern Europe*, edited by Torbjörn Bergman, Gabriella Ilonszki, and Wolfgang C. Müller, 252–302. Oxford: Oxford University Press.

Indridason, Indridi H., and Christopher J. Kam. 2008. "Cabinet Reshuffles and Ministerial Drift." *British Journal of Political Science* 38 (4): 621–56.

Kaarbo, Juliet. 1997. "Prime Minister Leadership Styles in Foreign Policy Decision-Making: A Framework for Research." *Political Psychology* 18 (3): 553–81.

Katz, Richard S. 1987. "Party Government and Its Alternatives." In *Party Governments: European and American Experiences*, edited by Richard S. Katz, 1–26. Florence: European University Institute.

King, Anthony. 1975. "Executives." In *Handbook of Political Science*, edited by Fred I. Greenstein and Nelson W. Polsby, 173–245. Glenview: Addison-Wesley Publishing Company.

King, Gary, James E. Alt, Nancy Elisabeth Burns, and Michael Laver. 1990. "A Unified Model of Cabinet Dissolution in Parliamentary Democracies." *American Journal of Political Science* 34 (3): 846–71.

Linek, Lukáš. 2014. "Czech Republic." *European Journal of Political Research Political Data Yearbook* 53 (1): 92–103.

Mainwaring, Scott, Carlos Gervasoni, and Annabella España-Najera. 2017. "Extra- and within-System Electoral Volatility." *Party Politics* 23 (6): 623–35.

Mair, Peter. 2008. "The Challenge to Party Government." *West European Politics* 31 (1–2): 211–34.

Müller-Rommel, Ferdinand, Corinna Kroeber, and Michelangelo Vercesi. 2020. "Political Careers of Ministers and Prime Ministers." In *The Oxford Handbook of Political Executives*, edited by Rudy B. Andeweg, Ludger Helms, Robert Elgie, Juliet Kaarbo, and Ferdinand Müller-Rommel, 229–50. Oxford: Oxford University Press.

Müller-Rommel, Ferdinand, Michelangelo Vercesi, and Jan Berz. 2022. *Prime Ministers in Europe. Changing Career Experiences and Profiles*. Cham: Palgrave Macmillan.

Müller, Wolfgang C. 2000. "Political Parties in Parliamentary Democracies: Making Delegation and Accountability Work." *European Journal of Political Research* 37: 309–33.

Müller, Wolfgang C., Torbjörn Bergman, and Kaare Strøm. 2008. "Coalition Theory and Cabinet Governance: An Introduction." In *Cabinets and Coalition Bargaining: The Democratic Life Cycle in Western Europe*, edited by Kaare Strøm, Wolfgang C. Müller, and Torbjörn Bergman, 1–50. Oxford: Oxford University Press.

Müller, Wolfgang C., and Wilfried Philipp. 1991. "Prime Ministers and Other Government Heads." In *The Profession of Government Minister in Western Europe*, edited by Jean Blondel and Jean-Louis Thiébault, 136–52. New York: St. Martin's Press.

Petrúšek, Ivan, and Aleš Kudrnáč. 2017. "Czech Republic." *European Journal of Political Research Political Data Yearbook* 56 (1): 70–78.

Poguntke, Thomas, and Paul Webb. 2005. "The Presidentialization of Politics in Democratic Societies: A Framework for Analysis." In *The Presidentialization of Politics: A Comparative Study of Modern Democracies*, edited by Thomas Poguntke and Paul Webb, 1–23. Oxford: Oxford University Press.

Protsyk, Oleh. 2006. "Intra-Executive Competition between President and Prime Minister: Patterns of Institutional Conflict and Cooperation under Semi-Presidentialism." *Political Studies* 54 (2): 219–44.

Saalfeld, Thomas. 2013. "Economic Performance, Political Institutions and Cabinet Durability in 28 European Parliamentary Democracies, 1945–2011." In *Party Governance and Party Democracy*, edited by Wolfgang C. Müller and Hanne Marthe Narud, 51–79. New York: Springer.

Samuels, David J., and Matthew S. Shugart. 2010. *Presidents, Parties, and Prime Ministers: How the Separation of Powers Affects Party Organization and Behavior*. Cambridge: Cambridge University Press.

Savage, Lee. 2018. "How and When Do Presidents Influence the Duration of Coalition Bargaining in Semi-Presidential Systems?" *European Journal of Political Research* 57 (2): 308–32.

Schleiter, Petra, and Edward Morgan-Jones. 2009. "Constitutional Power and Competing Risks: Monarchs, Presidents, Prime Ministers, and the Termination of East and West European Cabinets." *American Political Science Review* 103 (3): 496–512.

Shugart, Matthew Søberg, and John M. Carey. 1992. *Presidents and Assemblies: Constitutional Design and Electoral Dynamics*. Cambridge: Cambridge University Press.

Somer-Topcu, Zeynep, and Laron K. Williams. 2008. "Survival of the Fittest? Cabinet Duration in Postcommunist Europe." *Comparative Politics* 40 (3): 313–29.

Ştefan, Laurenţiu. 2020. "Party Leaders vs . Technocrats." *Communist and Post-Communist Studies* 53 (2): 47–60.

Strangio, Paul, Paul 't Hart, and James Walter. 2013. "Prime Ministers and the Performance of Public Leadership." In *Understanding Prime-Ministerial Performance: Comparative Perspectives*, edited by Paul Strangio, Paul 't Hart, and James Walter, 45–66. Oxford: Oxford University Press.

Tavits, Margit. 2008. "Party Systems in the Making: The Emergence and Success of New Parties in New Democracies." *British Journal of Political Science* 38 (1): 113–33.

Tzelgov, Eitan. 2011. "Communist Successor Parties and Government Survival in Central Eastern Europe." *European Journal of Political Research* 50 (4): 530–58.

Walther, Daniel, and Johan Hellström. 2022. "Government Termination in Europe: A Sensitivity Analysis." *West European Politics* 45 (3): 591–611.

Warwick, Paul. 1994. *Government Survival in Parliamentary Democracies*. Cambridge: Cambridge University Press.

Weller, Patrick. 1985. *First among Equals: Prime Ministers in Westminster Systems*. Sydney: Allen & Unwin.

———. 2014. "The Variability of Prime Ministers." In *The Oxford Handbook of Political Leadership*, edited by R.A.W. Rhodes and Paul 't Hart, 489–502. Oxford: Oxford University Press.

Winter, Lieven De. 1991. "Parliamentary and Party Pathways to the Cabinet." In *The Profession of Government Minister in Western Europe*, edited by Jean Blondel and Jean-Louis Thiébault, 44–69. London: Palgrave Macmillan.

Zuba, Krzysztof. 2020. "Leaders without Leadership: Surrogate Governments in Poland." *Europe-Asia Studies* 72 (1): 33–54.

Coping with the new party challenge: patterns of prime ministerial survival in Croatia and Slovenia

Dario Nikić Čakar ⓘ and Alenka Krašovec

ABSTRACT
The recent surge of genuinely new parties (GNPs) in Central and Eastern Europe has made the political environment of prime ministers (PMs) more difficult, by increasing uncertainty in coalition governance. We explore the survival strategies of PMs when dealing with GNPs in government. Focusing on cases from Croatia and Slovenia, we demonstrate that patterns of PM survival do not systematically differ depending on whether the PM comes from GNPs or established parties. Rather, PMs employed various strategies of cabinet conflict management and reshuffling party governments, with effective party leadership identified as the crucial factor for PMs to remain in office.

Introduction

In comparison to their counterparts in Western Europe, coalition governments in Central and Eastern Europe (CEE) are exhibiting lower levels of stability. The same applies to prime ministers (PMs) in the region, who have been described as rather weak and ineffective chief executives (Baylis 2007). Although the importance of PMs as political leaders has been widely recognised, few studies have explored PM survival in CEE (Müller-Rommel 2005; Baylis 2007; Grotz and Weber 2017).

In recent years, PMs in the region have faced additional challenges to the security of their tenure with the rise of genuinely new parties (GNPs), which are characterised as defying new actors usually born outside the conventional political arenas (Sikk 2005). The surge of GNPs has transformed the political environment in which PMs operate, since the inclusion of GNPs in coalition governments brings uncertainty and unpredictability to their stability, making PMs' positions as chief executives more vulnerable and fragile. The extant literature has not explored the relationship between PMs and GNPs in governments, focusing instead on other aspects of electoral and executive politics when dealing with the impact of new parties (Sikk 2005, 2012; Tavits 2008; Grotz and Weber 2017).

Our study aims to partially fill this research gap by exploring patterns of PM survival in Croatia and Slovenia, as these two countries recently witnessed electorally successful GNPs participating in government coalitions under different PMs. GNPs in both countries attracted significant shares of votes by raising strong criticisms against established parties and political elites. Moreover, they played the leading role in government formation, though with different modalities – in Croatia the GNP *The Bridge of Independent Lists* (Most) participated in coalition governments as a junior partner, while in Slovenia the GNPs *List of Zoran Janković–Positive Slovenia* (LZJ-PS) and *Party of Miro Cerar* (SMC) were the largest parties in their respective coalition governments, with PMs originating from them. At the same time, patterns of prime-ministerial survival varied within both countries, as some PMs who were facing GNPs in government had to leave office very early while others succeeded in remaining in office (almost) for the entire electoral term.

Against this background, we ask which factors explain the different survival success of PMs when GNPs are included in coalition governments. We generally argue that PMs may adopt different strategies at the cabinet and coalition levels to ensure their survival when GNPs challenge their standing as chief executives, but they also heavily rely on individual power resources like effective party leadership and political experience. In order to explore the impact of these factors on the varying survival success of PMs, we have selected two pairs of PMs in each country, namely Tihomir Orešković and Andrej Plenković in Croatia and Alenka Bratušek and Miro Cerar in Slovenia, foremost because they were the only PMs in both countries who had to deal with GNPs in their party governments. There were also some other PMs, particularly Slovenian Janša (2012–2013) and Pahor (2008–2011), who ran coalition governments with new parties included as junior partners, but we omitted them from the analysis as these parties fail to fit the criteria of genuineness (Sikk 2005).

In the next section, we present a theoretical framework for studying prime-ministerial survival when confronted with GNPs in government. In the second and third sections, we turn to the cases of Croatia and Slovenia, respectively, showing within-country patterns of prime-ministerial survival and identifying factors that help to explain the success of PMs in remaining in office. The final section highlights the major findings and reflects on their implications beyond the selected cases.

Strategies of prime-ministerial survival and the new party challenge

Many analyses in the field of executive governance are focused on explaining government duration in various political and social contexts. However, only a handful of studies have explored the survival of PMs as part of overall government stability (Strøm, Müller, and Bergman 2008). This individual-centred approach has proved to be especially important in the new democracies of CEE (Müller-Rommel 2005; Baylis 2007), given the high party-system instability and frequent government turnovers across the region. The puzzling nature of prime-ministerial survival in CEE is reflected in the contrasting patterns of government and prime-ministerial duration, as PMs are on average more durable than their party governments (Blondel, Müller-Rommel, and Malova 2007; Grotz and Weber 2017). There is, however, considerable within- and cross-country variation in this regard (see the Introduction to this Special Issue).

In the recent past, the survival of PMs in CEE has become even more critical as substantial changes within the party systems have raised GNPs to national prominence in several countries (Sikk 2005, 2012; Deschouwer 2008; Tavits 2006, 2008). When GNPs are included in government, they can be considered a particular challenge for prime-ministerial survival, as their inexperience and ideological indeterminacy could make them more inclined to sabotage joint cabinet decision-making and undermine the position of the chief executive (Deschouwer 2008; Grotz and Weber 2016). However, despite their general disadvantages in terms of predictability of behaviour, GNPs are sometimes included in coalition governments. After the elections, they may emerge as either the largest party with the biggest potential to form a government or as a pivotal party in coalition formation. Therefore, GNPs may significantly affect the stability of both PMs and their coalition governments, which is why special attention has to be paid to the ways in which PMs deal with GNPs in their cabinets.

What factors contribute to the survival of PMs challenged by GNPs in their government? We argue that PMs have different strategic options at two distinct levels: the *party coalition level* and the *cabinet level*. By strategy we mean the actions that PMs can employ to ensure their survival by containing challenges and threats that arise when faced with GNPs. At the party coalition level, PMs may employ government reshuffles as a mechanism of retaining power when faced with the threat to their survival posed by GNPs (Kam and Indriđason 2005; Indriđason and Kam 2008). Along this strategy, PMs may either reshuffle the cabinet by replacing certain ministers and/or change its partisan composition to restore cohesion within their coalition. If faced with intra-coalition conflicts caused by unpredictable behaviour of GNPs, reshuffling the cabinet or forming a new coalition government could be considered an effective strategy. However, as PMs risk ending up without majority support in parliament after replacing coalition parties, this strategy is the most hazardous for their survival and therefore not frequently used.

At the cabinet level, PMs are the dominant actors in charge of preventing and resolving intra-cabinet conflicts that threaten to end their office tenure prematurely (Andeweg and Timmermans 2008; Damgaard 2008; Saalfeld 2009; Bowler et al. 2016). To do so, PMs can rely on different mechanisms of conflict management that are the indicators of survival strategy at the cabinet level. *Formal mechanisms* are largely institutionalised bodies, such as cabinet committees or coalition committees, which meet regularly to discuss day-to-day politics and in which PMs are usually at the top of the decision-making chain, determining their content and structure. *Informal mechanisms* are usually ad hoc and called by PMs to resolve a potential threat to cabinet survival (e.g. bilateral negotiations with other leaders of coalition parties). Relying on these conflict management mechanisms can be considered the most accessible and least costly strategy for PMs when trying to ensure their survival, mostly because they can settle conflicts within their coalition without the need to invest additional resources.

In addition to the strategies at the coalition and cabinet levels, PMs may also rely on certain *individual power resources* that appear to be highly relevant for their survival, foremost party leadership and political experience. These power resources enable PMs to pursue one or the other strategy, as these strategies differ in their level of risk. Grotz and Weber (2017) argue that PMs who are party leaders or have accumulated cabinet experience have a higher propensity to survive longer in office than PMs who lack these traits. From our standpoint, the term "party leadership" has a very precise meaning in this article, as it exclusively refers to "holding a position of party leader", rather than to any more abstract notion of political leadership. Being a party leader can be valuable for PMs, since "the key resource available to the prime minister is leadership of a unitary, centralised, and disciplined parliamentary party" (Heffernan 2003, 354; see also Clemens 1998).[1] Effective party leadership implies not only strong control imposed by autonomous PMs on their parties (Poguntke and Webb 2005; Bennister 2012), but also a high standing and popularity that PMs enjoy in their parties which back them in office (Heffernan 2005; Strangio, 't Hart, and Walter 2013). Furthermore, political experience acquired in national politics and inter-party relations, particularly when previously holding government positions, can make it easier for PMs to organise cabinet decision-making and also effectively resolve intra-coalition conflicts (Grotz and Weber 2017).

To explore how PMs succeed in surviving in office when faced with GNPs in government, we formulate three assumptions. First, although individual power resources contribute to PMs' survival success, they may also interact with PMs' survival strategies at the coalition and cabinet levels. More precisely, power resources seem to be a precondition for the successful application of survival strategies at both levels. For instance, PMs who are strong party leaders may secure the backing of powerful allies within their parties, which can, in turn, increase their success in replacing troublemaking coalition partners. Similarly, previous experience in national politics, combined with in-depth understanding of complex relations between national parties, enable PMs to apply conflict-management mechanisms more effectively, particularly when informally negotiating with other party leaders over coalition survival. Second, there is a functional sequence between the survival strategies, i.e. PMs will first employ intra-cabinet conflict management because of its lower costs before they attempt to reshuffle the government as a high-cost strategy. Third, there is a difference in the effectiveness of survival strategies, as we expect the change of partisan composition of the cabinet to be the most effective strategy for PMs to remain in office.

In order to test these assumptions, Croatia and Slovenia seem to be appropriate cases. In both countries, GNPs have recently emerged as a salient feature of party systems, riding on a wave of general dissatisfaction with the performance of the economy and democracy. Moreover, they have been included in coalition governments. Therefore, we can explore how PMs in two similar contexts managed to survive with GNPs in government. At the same time, the case selection should also allow for sufficient variation between two countries, since Croatian PMs faced GNPs in government as junior coalition partners, while in Slovenia PMs came from GNPs which emerged as the largest parties after the two recent elections.

Patterns of prime-ministerial survival in Croatia

When assessing the patterns of prime-ministerial survival in Croatia, we broadly differentiate between two periods. The first includes the single-party rule during the 1990s, when prime-ministerial survival was exclusively dependent upon the will of a powerful president who exercised his broad prerogatives in a democratically deficient regime (Čular 2000; Čular and Nikić Čakar 2019). The second period begins with the constitutional reform in 2000, when democracy consolidated and coalition governments became the norm. In this context, PMs have faced a somewhat different and more challenging environment, with major threats to their survival coming from fragile parliamentary majorities in a fragmented multi-party system (Kasapović 2005). The following analysis focuses on the latter period only.

Table 1 shows that there were six PMs and thirteen cabinets in Croatia from 2000 to 2019. Eight cabinets had minority status, while only three were formed as minimal-winning coalitions and two as oversized coalitions. Furthermore, Croatian cabinets lasted on average for 535 days, with a broad range between the most durable one led by Milanović (1416 days) and the shortest one led by Plenković II (43 days). On the other hand, PMs have remained in office much longer than their party governments – 993 days on average. However, their office duration varies almost as much as that of their cabinets. The longest-serving PM was Sanader with 1968 days, while the shortest-serving PM Orešković managed to stay in office for only 146 days. Interestingly, Orešković and Plenković have been the only PMs who had to deal with a GNP in their coalition government. Even at first glance, it is quite clear that they had very different success when faced with the new party challenge. In the following, we are unravelling the mechanisms behind their efforts to survive in office with a GNP in government.

In both the 2015 and 2016 parliamentary elections, two new parties – Most and Živi zid (Human Shield) – raised strong anti-establishment and populist demands against established parties and mobilised significant voter support. Their breakthrough has radically altered the Croatian party system, as they obtained a significant share of parliamentary seats (Nikić Čakar and Raos 2015, 2016). Both parties might be labelled GNPs, since they were born outside of the conventional political arenas. Although at least one new

Table 1. Prime ministers and party governments in Croatia (2000–2019).

Cabinet	Date in	Date out	PM duration [a]	Cabinet duration [a]	Party composition [b]	Cabinet type [c]
Račan I	2000-01-27	2001-06-04	1371	494	**SDP**-HSLS-HNS-HSS-IDS-LS	sur
Račan II	2001-06-04	2002-07-05		396	**SDP**-HSLS-HNS-HSS-LS	sur
Račan III	2002-07-30	2003-11-23		481	**SDP**-Libra-HNS-HSS-LS	min
Sanader I	2003-12-23	2006-02-09	1433	779	**HDZ**-DC	min
Sanader II	2006-02-09	2007-11-25		654	**HDZ**	min
Sanader III	2008-01-13	2009-07-01	535	535	**HDZ**-HSS-HSLS-SDSS	mwc
Kosor I	2009-07-06	2010-07-10	881	369	**HDZ**-HSS-HSLS-SDSS	mwc
Kosor II	2010-07-10	2011-12-04		512	**HDZ**-HSS-SDSS	min
Milanović	2011-12-23	2015-11-08	1416	1416	**SDP**-HNS-IDS	mwc
Orešković	2016-01-22	2016-06-16	146	146	**I**[d]-HDZ-Most	min
Plenković I	2016-10-19	2017-04-27	1168	190	**HDZ**-Most	min
Plenković II	2017-04-27	2017-06-09		43	**HDZ**	min
Plenković III	2017-06-09			935 [e]	**HDZ**-HNS	min

Source: Authors' compilation. Cabinets with GNPs are highlighted in grey.
[a]The horizontal lines demarcate parliamentary terms. Office duration in days.
[b]Party of PM marked in bold; parties ordered by parliamentary size.
[c]MIN-minority; MWC-minimal winning coalition; SUR-surplus.
[d]Independent PM nominated by HDZ.
[e]Duration counted until 31 December 2019.

party has appeared in every election since 1990, they have been created mostly as a splinter from established parties and have not been particularly successful in surviving in the political arena (Nikić Čakar and Čular 2016). Against this background, Most and Živi zid aimed at transforming the bipolar structure of party competition in Croatia, which previously significantly restricted the electoral potential of new parties, presenting them with a choice to approach one of two opposing ideological camps or to stay out of the bloc competition and wither away (Henjak 2018).

The GNPs' electoral success in 2015 and 2016 left the two traditional party camps in a deadlock situation, as for the first time neither managed to set up a viable coalition. This enabled Most to become the pivotal party in government formation. While calling for purification of Croatian political parties, overburdened with corruption and clientelism, Most initiated simultaneous negotiations with the two opposing blocks after the 2015 election, aiming to create a grand coalition with two leading parties, HDZ and SDP (Nikić Čakar and Raos 2016). After a lengthy bargaining process full of thriller-style twists and turns, Most broke off a deal with SDP and finalised a deal with the HDZ-led coalition, forming a minority government supported in parliament by two other smaller parties. A similar scenario re-emerged after the 2016 parliamentary election, only this time it was much easier for HDZ and Most to build a joint government, with HDZ and its new leader Plenković determining the dynamics of coalition negotiations. Another two-party minority government was formed, supported again in parliament by several smaller parties, including representatives of ethnic minorities.[2]

Additionally, an insight into coalition governance since 2000 reveals that conflict-management mechanisms were not formally institutionalised by coalition or cabinet committees. Instead, they were set up as rather informal rules of the game, dependent upon mutual personal understandings of coalition party leaders and their behind-the-scenes wheeling and dealing (Nikić Čakar 2020). In particular, PMs Račan, Sanader and Milanović mostly relied on direct bilateral negotiations to deal with conflicts that threatened their survival in office.[3] This personalised strategy for resolving intra-coalition disputes was built around the narrow circle of the respective party leaders and the PM as central actor, with limited opportunity for public and party scrutiny. For instance, Račan mostly relied on personal relations with other coalition leaders. Similarly, Sanader and Milanović were usually discussing coalition politics and making initial policy decisions with other coalition leaders over private lunches or in some other informal manner.

Against this contextual background, the remainder of this section analyses how successful PMs Orešković and Plenković were in surviving in office when faced with the inclusion of GNP Most in their cabinets.[4] When Most ended up in a coalition with HDZ after the 2015 election, the two government parties selected the independent technocrat Orešković as PM. Orešković was unknown to the Croatian public, as he grew up abroad and built his career in the international pharmaceutical sector. He did not have any party background and was completely inexperienced in politics. Soon this proved to be his crucial handicap for surviving in PM office, coupled with serious disputes raging between HDZ and Most. Intra-coalition conflicts were especially evident in the relationship between the party leaders Tomislav Karamarko (HDZ) and Božo Petrov (Most), who were acting as deputy PMs at the same time. Although HDZ and Most established a special body called the Council for Cooperation to oversee coalition coordination, this proved to be completely ineffectual in resolving internal conflicts. Orešković was excluded from making important decisions right from the start, as Karamarko and Petrov preferred to settle all contested issues in bilateral behind-the-scenes meetings. When their personal animosities threatened to bring down the cabinet, Orešković tried to mediate between them but failed, given his inexperience and unfamiliarity with running political affairs.

The final blow to the prospects of the PM to survive came with the unpredictable behaviour of Most. This led to an intra-coalition paralysis, as severe clashes and mutual sabotages between HDZ and Most undermined the stability of the cabinet, which was heading towards its genetically preprogrammed suicide (Raos 2016). Orešković persistently refused to resign, eventually making a desperate move to reshuffle the cabinet by asking Karamarko and Petrov to resign instead. The attempt failed due to the PM's inexperience and the lack of any control over the HDZ, which turned its back on him. Karamarko also tried to stabilise the government by restructuring its partisan composition but failed on his own. The government was finally terminated by a vote of no confidence initiated by the HDZ, which was the first time in modern Croatian history that a government lost the confidence of its own parliamentary majority.

HDZ and Most gave their coalition marriage another chance after early parliamentary elections in September 2016. This time, Most lost some of its electoral popularity and parliamentary strength, while HDZ gained additional support mostly due to the personalised electoral effect of its new leader Plenković. To strengthen the stability of the government, Plenković negotiated individual coalition agreements with several smaller parties, including the representatives of ethnic minorities, who decided to support the coalition on a contractual basis. Such a "backup plan" was to be used in case of conflicts with Most, which was confirmed in the upcoming period.

Compared to his predecessor, Plenković is perceived by interviewees as a strong party leader and PM involved in the policy-making process of every cabinet portfolio. Besides that, Plenković has sought to resolve all conflicts that threatened the survival of the coalition government in bilateral and informal talks with Petrov, who was appointed as the speaker of the parliament. However, this second coalition did not last long, given that Most once again proved to be an unreliable partner. The Most ministers "continued to disapprove and criticize major government initiatives coming from HDZ ministers or Plenković himself, behaving almost as some sort of opposition to its own government" (Nikić Čakar and Raos 2018, 54). The culmination of intra-coalition tensions came only several months after the government was inaugurated, when opposition parties initiated a motion of no confidence against the Minister of Finance over his involvement in a high-profile politico-economic affair. When the Most ministers, contrary to Plenković's instructions, voted for the motion of no confidence, he unilaterally decided to dismiss them and ended the coalition.

Although these dramatic events threatened the PM survival, Plenković instantly activated his backup plan to avoid early election. His strategy was directed towards forming a new and previously inconceivable coalition with the HNS that was considered the most loyal coalition partner of the left-wing SDP, thus breaking the traditional ideological barriers. Plenković managed to secure the backing of HDZ for this move and also the support of some smaller parties, creating an extremely heterogeneous and apparently unstable parliamentary majority. However, despite all the challenges that came along, the new coalition government has proved to be rather stable and resistant, with very promising prospects for Plenković to survive as PM for the entire constitutional term.

When comparing Orešković and Plenković, we clearly observe the theoretically expected patterns. While both PMs faced a highly challenging context resulting from the government inclusion of the inexperienced and anti-establishment Most, the outcomes were substantially different. On the one hand, Orešković had no particular prospect to survive in office as an independent PM: he was left out from organising parliamentary support for the coalition government at the beginning; he was marginalised and uninfluential in resolving intra-coalition conflicts; and he completely failed to reshuffle the cabinet. On the other hand, Plenković was much more successful in employing strategic options to survive: he negotiated broader parliamentary support for his government; he was effective in resolving intra-coalition conflicts up to the point when insurmountable differences between the coalition parties emerged; and he successfully rearranged the partisan composition of the cabinet by forming a new coalition across the ideological aisle.

Several factors explain these differences in survival success. First, the two PMs had a completely different political experience prior to assuming office, with Orešković being a total outsider to national politics, while Plenković spent his entire career in politics in various positions. Second, Orešković was acting as an independent PM, without any party background to support his survival efforts, while Plenković was firmly in control of his party, which made his survival much easier and more effective. Finally, the formal support of some smaller parliamentary parties for changing the composition of the government proved to be an important factor in explaining why Plenković successfully survived the coalition breakup with Most, while Orešković failed to arrange this kind of a backup plan and lost his ground immediately after the coalition government fell apart.

Patterns of prime-ministerial survival in Slovenia

Although the constitutional framework of Slovenia has remained largely unchanged since 1991, the country has seen divergent patterns of survival of PMs and party governments. As Table 2 shows, all post-electoral governments have been formed as minimal-winning or surplus coalitions except for the cabinet led by Marjan Šarec that was built up by a minority coalition of five parties. There have been altogether nine different PMs and nineteen cabinets. Some PMs, foremost Janez Drnovšek, have managed to survive longer than their governments. Drnovšek stayed in office altogether for 3459 days, while PMs' average duration in Slovenia is 762 days. This is still much more than the duration of governments, which have survived for 524 days on average. However, only the Janša I cabinet survived for the entire legislative term with its initial party composition.

In Slovenia, the emergence of new parliamentary parties has been a constant feature of the party system since the democratic transition. These parties were mostly formed due to mergers or splits of existing parties, or by previously established politicians, and were rather small (Fink-Hafner and Krašovec 2013). However, since the 2011 parliamentary election a new phenomenon of very successful GNPs has emerged, building their support on anti-establishment and anti-corruption rhetoric. Several factors contributed to this rise of GNPs: the disintegration of the predominant liberal party (LDS) after 2004; the economic and financial crisis in 2009 and the inability of established parties to deal with it properly; increasing levels of citizen dissatisfaction due to corruption and declining trust in politics

Table 2. Prime ministers and party governments in Slovenia (1990–2019).

Cabinet	Date in	Date out	PM duration [a]	Cabinet duration [a]	Party composition [b]	Cabinet type [c]
Peterle	1990-05-16	1992-04-22	707	707	**SKD,** SLS, SDZ, ZS, SDS, LS	mwc
Drnovšek I	1992-05-14	1992-12-06	206	206	**LDS**, SDP, SDZ, ZS, SDS, SSS	sur
Drnovšek II	1993-01-25	1994-03-29	1385	428	**LDS**, SKD, ZLSD, SDS	sur
Drnovšek III	1994-03-29	1996-01-31		673	**LDS**, SKD, ZLSD	mwc
Drnovšek IV	1996-01-31	1996-11-10		284	**LDS**, SKD	min
Drnovšek V	1997-02-27	2000-04-08	1136	1136	**LDS**, SLS, DeSUS	mwc
Bajuk	2000-06-07	2000-10-15	130	130	**SLS**, SDS, SKD	min
Drnovšek VI	2000-11-30	2002-12-02	732	732	**LDS**, ZLSD, SLS+SKD, DeSUS	sur
Rop I	2002-12-19	2004-04-04	654	472	**LDS**, ZLSD, SLS+SKD, DeSUS	sur
Rop II	2004-04-04	2004-10-03		182	**LDS**, ZLSD, DeSUS	mwc
Janša I	2004-12-03	2008-09-21	1388	1388	**SDS**, NSi, SLS, DeSUS	mwc
Pahor I	2008-11-21	2011-05-09	1033	899	**SD**, Zares, DeSUS, LDS	mwc
Pahor II	2011-05-09	2011-06-27		49	**SD**, Zares, LDS	min
Pahor III	2011-06-27	2011-09-20		85	**SD**, LDS	min
Janša II	2012-02-10	2013-01-23	378	348	**SDS**, DL, DeSUS, SLS, NSi	sur
Janša III	2013-01-23	2013-02-22		30	**SDS**, DeSUS, SLS, NSi	min
Bratušek	2013-03-20	2014-05-05	411	411	**PS**, SD, DL, DeSUS	mwc
Cerar	2014-09-18	2018-03-14	1273	1273	**SMC**, DeSUS, SD	sur
Šarec	2018-09-13		474	474 [d]	**LMŠ**, SD, SMC, SAB, DeSUS	min

Source: Authors' compilation. Cabinets with GNPs are highlighted in grey.
[a]The horizontal lines demarcate parliamentary terms. Office duration in days.
[b]Party of PM marked in bold; parties ordered by parliamentary size.
[c]MIN-minority; MWC-minimal winning coalition; SUR-surplus.
[d]Duration counted until 31 December 2019.

and established parties (Haughton and Krašovec 2013; Krašovec et al. 2014; Krašovec and Johannsen 2016).

The emergence of GNPs has also led to a different government status of newcomer parties. Prior to 2011, established parties were willing to grant newcomers a status of junior coalition partner or just a supporting party (Krašovec and Krpič 2019a). From the groundbreaking 2011 election on, GNPs were the largest government parties and their leaders became PMs. PMs Bratušek and Cerar are cases under investigation in this article. Although the present government has been formed by GNP–List of Marjan Šarec and led by its leader Šarec, we are not going to include it in the analysis since at the time of writing the article this coalition government was still in power.

Although the LZJ-PS received the largest share of votes in the 2011 elections, its leader Zoran Janković failed to form a coalition government. His main opponent Janez Janša

(Slovenian Democratic Party–SDS) succeeded in this endeavour, but his government was brought down after one year by a corruption scandal involving both Janša and Janković. At the same time, Slovenia experienced protests during 2012 which were inspired by anger over political corruption and mismanagement of the fiscal and economic crises (Fink-Hafner and Krašovec 2014).

As the Troika (European Commission, European Central Bank and IMF) threatened to intervene in Slovenian internal affairs (Fink-Hafner and Krašovec 2014, 285), a new coalition government was formed by Janković's protégé Bratušek, who also became the acting leader of the PS.

In the 2014 parliamentary election, several GNPs pushed a very strong anti-corruption rhetoric, raising critical voices in favour of conducting politics differently and emphasising the rule of law as the most important topic (Krašovec and Haughton 2014). Among these GNPs was the SMC, of the politically inexperienced university professor Cerar, that was formed just before the election and received 34.5% of the support. In the aftermath, the SMC formed a coalition government with two established parties as junior partners.

In the sections below we pay special attention to the strategies of PMs coming from GNPs, Bratušek and Cerar, applied to survival in their office, describing at the same time some contextual background with their predecessors in this regard. Following the theoretical part, our attention will be focused on both levels of the strategies that can be used by the PMs: party coalition level and cabinet level.

At the cabinet level, we can say that even before the instability engulfed the party system in 2011, PMs in Slovenia had successfully employed formal conflict-management mechanisms (Andeweg and Timmermans 2008). All governments except for Peterle, Drnovšek I and Bajuk had coalition agreements that also addressed the topic of conflict-management mechanisms (Krašovec and Krpič 2019a). Generally speaking, PMs were much more prone to prevent conflicts within coalitions than to set up conflict-resolution mechanisms. Krašovec and Krpič (2019b) argue that in the period before the rise of GNPs, coalition partners mostly relied on regular meetings of party and parliamentary party leaders as the most frequent conflict-management mechanism.

Sometimes PMs insisted on direct involvement in conflict resolution, especially in cases of disagreements between ministers. Drnovšek was inclined to let ministers handle disagreements by themselves, and ministers were usually pushed to find a solution before the government meeting; otherwise, he would make a final decision. On the other hand, Janša was frequently deciding on his own without postponing the issue until the next meeting (Krašovec 2008). Pahor tried to mediate between ministers in such situations but often was unsuccessful in performing his coordination or arbitral tasks (Krašovec and Krpič 2019a). Personal conflicts were rather rare to find in coalitions until 2011, while policy conflicts took place (almost) regardless of the ideological distance between coalition partners (Krašovec and Krpič 2019a).

PM Bratušek did not extensively use cabinet-level survival strategies, as exposed by two interviewees, although these mechanisms were at her disposal according to the coalition agreement. However, Bratušek decided to reshuffle the cabinet several times, but only exchanged some ministers mostly due to personal scandals and not the partisan composition of the cabinet (Fink-Hafner and Krašovec 2014). According to interviewees, Bratušek benefited from the external environment, especially the threat of the Troika arrival, which united coalition parties in focusing on stabilising the Slovenian fiscal and financial system. On the other hand, Bratušek continuously faced serious problems within her own party. As acting leader of the PS, she faced strong pressure coming from the party's founding father Janković, who was trying to influence the government's decisions to a large extent. When this personal conflict intensified, it led to the battle over the party leadership position in 2014, coupled with warnings of junior coalition partners that they would leave the government if Janković regained the leadership. Once he succeeded in winning back the party leadership, Bratušek decided to resign, thus triggering early election.

PM Cerar started his office term in a context of major political and economic instability. Therefore, he decided to strengthen his position by forming a surplus coalition with the Social Democrats (SD) and the Democratic Party of Pensioners of Slovenia (DeSUS). With this move, he followed a similar survival strategy employed by Drnovšek in the 1990s. Additionally, Cerar overcompensated his coalition partners in the portfolio distribution to stabilise the parliamentary majority (Krašovec 2015). At the party coalition level, he followed a similar strategy of cabinet reshuffles as his predecessors, focusing primarily on scandal-ridden ministers. He exchanged ministers in almost half of the portfolios, in some of them even several times (Krašovec 2015, 2016).

Three interviewees pointed out that PM Cerar relied on an elaborated coalition agreement in cabinet governance, including conflict-management mechanisms that were included mostly due to his political inexperience. The reliance on these formal mechanisms helped him in coping with intra-coalitional conflicts. As one interviewee stressed, the insistence on precise rules gave PM Cerar and his party formal power over the other coalition partners. In a similar vein as previous PMs, he also engaged in informal and bilateral meetings with leaders of coalition partners.

Cerar was also pursuing a consensual leadership style vis-à-vis his coalition partners, even though the public perceived him as an ineffective and indecisive leader. Additionally, he did not hesitate in soliciting and following the advice of his more experienced coalition partners. In this way, his survival strategies show how the lack of political experience can be compensated with speedy learning. For example, in the coalition negotiation process, Cerar was very open towards his coalition partners' preferences, while in the past the leaders of the largest government parties were more inclined to prioritise their own ideas. However, despite very functional conflict-management mechanisms, as well as cabinet reshuffles, tensions among the coalition parties were too strong for Cerar to complete his term, so he decided to resign several months before the end of the term.

When comparing Bratušek and Cerar, their differential success in surviving emerges from different strategies at the party coalition level. While Cerar formed a surplus coalition, Bratušek formed "only" a minimal-winning coalition. However, there are two additional factors explaining their different success. First, Cerar benefited from the fact that he was, contrary to Bratušek, firmly in control of his party as "real" party leader. Second, the international environment in which Bratušek had to operate was much more demanding, yet it homogenised coalition partners, although just for one year.

Conclusion

PMs are the key players in party governments. Hence, it is essential to study how they survive in office and which strategies they employ to do so. Their survival efforts are particularly burdened with the challenges posed by GNPs, as they bring additional uncertainty into coalition governance. The analysis of four PMs in Croatia and Slovenia shows that there are differentiated patterns of prime-ministerial survival with GNPs in government. Plenković and Cerar stand out as successful PMs in terms of their survival, while Orešković and Bratušek can be characterised as rather ineffective in securing their office.

Plenković and Cerar successfully engaged survival strategies that are traditionally at PMs' disposal at both the coalition and cabinet levels. They arranged broader parliamentary support for their governments during the coalition formation and were effective in handling intra-coalition conflicts by using informal (Plenković) and formal (Cerar) mechanisms of coalition management. The major difference in their survival attempts concerns the use of government reshuffles. When intra-coalition conflicts with Most became overwhelming, Plenković successfully rearranged the partisan composition of the cabinet by moving beyond ideological cleavages to attract a new coalition partner. Faced with similar intra-coalition conflicts with junior partners, the politically inexperienced Cerar avoided restructuring the partisan composition and opted for an early election instead.

On the other hand, Orešković and Bratušek proved to be largely unsuccessful in securing their survival in office, as they did not get along well with the GNPs in government and were forced to step down too early. Their survival strategies almost completely failed. For different reasons, they did not negotiate broader partisan support for their governments. Furthermore, due to their political inexperience, they were generally ineffective in dealing with intra-coalition conflicts, although Bratušek was somewhat more successful given the external pressure. Finally, they were left without any options to rearrange the cabinet composition.

Our findings demonstrate that the functional sequence of survival strategies plays a significant role in explaining patterns of PM behaviour when faced with the challenge of GNPs. PMs in both countries were inclined to first employ a low-cost conflict-management strategy. When this strategy proved ineffective, as the Croatian case shows, they applied a high-cost strategy of changing the partisan composition of the cabinet. As our findings suggest, this approach proved to be much more effective in maintaining PMs in office compared to other strategies. Furthermore, political experience in general and effective party leadership in particular turned out to be crucial factors for PM survival. The cases of Orešković and Bratušek show that inexperienced PMs who accessed the chief-executive office without any party stronghold had no particular prospects of surviving for a longer time. Moreover, individual resources indeed work as a precondition for the successful employment of survival strategies at the coalition and cabinet levels, as demonstrated by the cases of Plenković (political experience and party leadership) and Cerar (party leadership and speedy learning).

We argue that this striking relationship between party leadership and PM survival could also pave the way for further research on patterns of PM survival in CEE countries. For instance, one could explore how the lack of a developed party structure, which is a basic characteristic of GNPs, affects the prospects of their leaders to remain in prime-ministerial office. Moreover, by taking into consideration the uncertainty and unpredictability that GNPs bring in coalition governance, scholars could also investigate how PMs from established parties develop new coalition-building strategies to cope with the challenge of GNPs. Are they going to rely more on building coalitions across ideological cleavages, and is there any other alternative strategy for them to escape GNPs in government? Furthermore, an additional question can also be exposed on how PMs from GNPs could

Notes

1. Contrary to the argument that leadership can be seen as a resource, some scholars argue that position-related resources are not possessed by a leader, but rather have to be successfully used in order to bring them to bear. In other words, a leader has to use particular leadership skills to benefit from the leadership position itself (Helms 2019).
2. Almost all Croatian governments since the mid-2000s have been supported, usually on a contractual basis, by ethnic minority representatives, which significantly contributes to their stability.
3. This empirical evidence is extracted from 13 interviews conducted with former ministers and PMs from the Račan I to the Milanović cabinets. In addition, we also analysed three coalition agreements for the Račan I, Sanader III and Milanović cabinets.
4. Our analysis is supported by evidence from interviews with six ministers in the Orešković and Plenković I–III cabinets, supplemented by examination of two coalition agreements and one government programme presented in the parliament.

Acknowledgments

We are very grateful to Florian Grotz and Marko Kukec for their invaluable comments and suggestions.

Disclosure statement

No potential conflict of interest was reported by the author(s).

ORCID

Dario Nikić Čakar http://orcid.org/0000-0001-9905-8066

References

Andeweg, R. B., and A. Timmermans. 2008. "Conflict Management in Coalition Government." In *Cabinets and Coalition Bargaining: The Democratic Life Cycle in Western Europe*, edited by K. Strøm, W. C. Müller, and T. Bergman, 269–300. Oxford: Oxford University Press.

PRIME MINISTERS AND PARTY GOVERNMENTS IN CENTRAL AND EASTERN EUROPE

Baylis, T. A. 2007. "Embattled Executives: Prime Ministerial Weakness in East Central Europe." *Communist and Post-Communist Studies* 40 (1): 81–106.

Bennister, M. 2012. *Prime Ministers in Power*. London: Palgrave Macmillan.

Blondel, J., F. Müller-Rommel, and D. Malova. 2007. *Governing New European Democracies*. New York: Palgrave Macmillan.

Bowler, S., T. Bräuninger, M. Debus, and I. H. Indriđason. 2016. "Let's Just Agree to Disagree: Dispute Resolution Mechanisms in Coalition Agreements." *The Journal of Politics* 78 (4): 1264–1278.

Clemens, C. 1998. "Party Management as a Leadership Resource: Kohl and the CDU/CSU." *German Politics* 7 (1): 91–119.

Čular, G. 2000. "Political Development in Croatia 1990–2000: Fast Transition – Postponed Consolidation." *Politička misao* 37 (5): 30–46.

Čular, G., and D. Nikić Čakar. 2019. "Institutionalisation of a Charismatic Movement Party: The Case of Croatian Democratic Union." In *Institutionalisation of Political Parties*, edited by R. Harmel, and L. G. Svasand, 171–192. London: ECPR Press/Rowman & Littlefield.

Damgaard, E. 2008. "Cabinet Termination." In *Coalition Governments in Western Europe*, edited by W. C. Müller, and K. Strøm, 301–326. Oxford: Oxford University Press.

Deschouwer, K. 2008. *New Parties in Government*. London: Routledge.

Fink-Hafner, D., and A. Krašovec. 2013. "Factors Affecting the Long-Term Success of New Parliamentary Parties: Findings in a Post-Communist Context." *Romanian Journal of Political Science* 13 (2): 40–68.

Fink-Hafner, D., and A. Krašovec. 2014. "Slovenia: Political Data Yearbook 2013." *European Journal of Political Research* 53 (1): 281–286.

Grotz, F., and T. Weber. 2016. "New Parties, Information Uncertainty, and Government Formation: Evidence from Central and Eastern Europe." *European Political Science Review* 8 (3): 449–472.

Grotz, F., and T. Weber. 2017. ""Prime Ministerial Tenure in Central and Eastern Europe: The Role of Party Leadership and Cabinet Experience"." In *Parties, Governments and Elites: The Comparative Study of Democracy*, edited by P. Harfst, I. Kubbe, and T. Poguntke, 229–248. Wiesbaden: Springer.

Haughton, T., and A. Krašovec. 2013. "The 2011 Parliamentary Elections in Slovenia." *Electoral Studies* 32 (1): 201–204.

Heffernan, R. 2003. "Prime Ministerial Predominance? Core Executive Politics in the UK." *The British Journal of Politics and International Relations* 5 (3): 347–372.

Heffernan, R. 2005. "Exploring (and Explaining) the British Prime Minister." *The British Journal of Politics and International Relations* 7: 605–620.

Helms, L. 2019. "When Less is More: 'Negative Resources' and the Performance of Presidents and Prime Ministers." *Politics* 39 (3): 269–283.

Henjak, A. 2018. "Lojalnost, glas ili izlazak: izborna participacija i potpora novim strankama u Hrvatskoj." *Anali Hrvatskog politološkog društva* 14 (1): 79–103.

Indriđason, I., and C. Kam. 2008. "Cabinet Reshuffles and Ministerial Drift." *British Journal of Political Science* 38 (4): 621–656.

Kam, C., and I. Indriđason. 2005. "The Timing of Cabinet Reshuffles in Five Westminster Parliamentary Systems." *Legislative Studies Quarterly* 30 (3): 327–363.

Kasapović, M. 2005. "Koalicijske vlade u Hrvatskoj: prva iskustva u komparativnoj perspektivi." In *Izbori i konsolidacija demokracije u Hrvatskoj*, edited by G. Čular, 181–209. Zagreb: Fakultet političkih znanosti.

Krašovec, A. 2008. "Evolution of (In)Formal Roles of the Prime Minister's Office and the General Secretariat of the Government in Slovenia." In *Politico-Administrative Relations at the Centre: Actors, Structures and Processes Supporting the Core Executive*, edited by B. Connaughton, G. Sootla, and G. Peters, 36–59. Bratislava: NISPAcee.

Krašovec, A. 2015. "Slovenia: Political Data Yearbook 2014." *European Journal of Political Research* 54 (1): 269–277.

Krašovec, A. 2016. "Slovenia: Political Data Yearbook 2015." *European Journal of Political Research* 55 (1): 237–243.

Krašovec, A., and T. Haughton. 2014. "Privlačnost novog: nove stranke i promjena stranačkog sustava u Sloveniji." *Političke analize* 5 (19): 48–53.

Krašovec, A., and L. Johannsen. 2016. "Recent Developments in Democracy in Slovenia." *Problems of Post-Communism* 63 (5-6): 313–322.

Krašovec, A., L. Johannsen, K. Hilmer Pedersen, and T. Deželan. 2014. "Nevarnost sistemske korupcije v Sloveniji: spodbude in ovire." *Revija za kriminalistiko in kriminologijo* 65 (3): 207–220.

Krašovec, A., and T. Krpič. 2019a. "Slovenia: Majority Coalitions and the Strategy of Dropping out of Cabinet." In *Coalition Governance in Central Eastern Europe*, edited by T. Bergman, G. Ilonszki, and W. C. Müller, 475–521. Oxford: Oxford University Press.

Krašovec, A., and T. Krpič. 2019b. "Naj ostanem ali grem? Vladne koalicije in koalicijski sporazumi v Sloveniji med letoma 1990 in 2018." *Teorija in praksa* 56 (1): 245–262.

Müller-Rommel, F. 2005. Types of Cabinet Durability in Central Eastern Europe. Available from: https://escholarship.org/uc/item/8cv4134w [Accessed 14 June 2019].

Nikić Čakar, D. 2020. "Croatia: Strong Prime Ministers and Weak Coalitions." In *Coalition Governance in Western Europe*, edited by T. Bergman, H. Bäck, and J. Hellström. Oxford: Oxford University Press, forthcoming.

Nikić Čakar, D., and G. Čular. 2016. "Organizational Structures of Political Parties in Croatia." In *Organizational Structures of Political Parties in Central and Eastern European Countries*, edited by K. Sobolevska-Myslik et al., 109–132. Krakow: Jagiellonian University Press.

Nikić Čakar, D., and V. Raos. 2015. "Croatia." *European Journal of Political Research Political Data Yearbook* 54 (1): 60–68.

Nikić Čakar, D., and V. Raos. 2016. "Croatia." *European Journal of Political Research Political Data Yearbook* 55 (1): 50–58.

Nikić Čakar, D., and V. Raos. 2018. "Croatia: Political Development and Data for 2017." *European Journal of Political Research Political Data Yearbook* 57 (1): 53–60.

Poguntke, T., and P. Webb, eds. 2005. *The Presidentialization of Politics*. Oxford: Oxford University Press.

Raos, V. 2016. A Pre-Programmed Suicide of a Government: The Fall of the Orešković Cabinet and Early Elections in Croatia. Available from: https://whogoverns.eu/a-pre-programmed-suicide-of-a-government-the-fall-of-the-oreskovic-cabinet-and-early-elections-in-croatia/ [Accessed 26 June 2019].

Saalfeld, T. 2009. "Intra-party Conflict and Cabinet Survival in 17 West European Democracies, 1945–1999." In *Intra-party Politics and Coalition Governments*, edited by D. Giannetti, and K. Benoit, 169–186. London: Routledge.

Sikk, A. 2005. "How Unstable? Volatility and the Genuinely New Parties in Eastern Europe." *European Journal of Political Research* 44 (3): 391–412.

Sikk, A. 2012. "Newness as a Winning Formula for New Political Parties." *Party Politics* 18 (4): 465–486.

Strangio, P., P. 't Hart, and J. Walter, eds. 2013. *Understanding Prime-Ministerial Performance*. Oxford: Oxford University Press.

Strøm, K., W. C. Müller, and T. Bergman, eds. 2008. *Cabinets and Coalition Bargaining: The Democratic Life Cycle in Western Europe*. Oxford: Oxford University Press.

Tavits, M. 2006. "Party System Change: Testing a Model of New Party Entry." *Party Politics* 12 (1): 99–119.

Tavits, M. 2008. "Party Systems in the Making: The Emergence and Success of New Parties in New Democracies." *British Journal of Political Science* 38 (1): 113–133.

∂ OPEN ACCESS

Juggling friends and foes: Prime Minister Borissov's surprise survival in Bulgaria

Maria Spirova and Radostina Sharenkova-Toshkova

ABSTRACT
Prime Ministers (PMs) in Central and Eastern Europe have been relatively weak, although substantial variation in the survival both within and across countries exists. In Bulgaria, Boyko Borissov came to power in 2009 in most unfavourable situation: leader of a new party, he faced minority situation in parliament and had to cope with an ideologically heterogeneous coalition. Still, Borissov has become the longest serving PM in the country. This article examines the cabinet governance of Borissov I, II and III explores the PM's relationship with other parties inside and outside parliament as well as the mechanisms of cabinet management.

Introduction

That Prime Ministers (PMs) in Central and Eastern Europe (CEE) have been relatively weak has emerged as a norm in the literature (Baylis 2007). Short tenure durations, unstable relations with the parliaments and tense balance of power with the heads of state are among the typical characteristics of PMs in the post-communist context. Their survival in chief executive office has generally been under the averages of their West European counterparts (Mueller-Rommel 2005). However, there is also substantial variation in prime-ministerial duration in CEE "both within and across individual countries" (Grotz and Weber 2017, 231). A plethora of "contextual, individual and institutional" factors might impact the longevity of the PMs, just as anywhere else in the world (Strangio et al. 2013, 5), such as their individual leadership potential, the nature of their relationship with the parliamentary parties and the political ambitions of the head of state. Further, if PMs are propelled into power by new parties, their tenure in office might become even more fraught with insecurity and uncertainty as new parties in government are particularly prone to lose votes, undergo ideological and leadership challenges, and identity change (Deschouwer 2008, 5).

In Bulgaria, Boyko Borissov accessed the PM office after his party, GERB, won the 2009 parliamentary elections as a newcomer to the national political scene. In the meantime, he has become the longest serving PM in the country having had three separate post-electoral cabinets. In many ways, he has succeeded to do so against all odds. In his first

---

This is an Open Access article distributed under the terms of the Creative Commons Attribution-NonCommercial-NoDerivatives License (http://creativecommons.org/licenses/by-nc-nd/4.0/), which permits non-commercial re-use, distribution, and reproduction in any medium, provided the original work is properly cited, and is not altered, transformed, or built upon in any way.

term, Borissov became PM as chairman of a new party built for the most part around his personality. His first two cabinets were minority governments that were reliant on the support of ideologically divergent parliamentary parties. Still, during both periods Borissov has managed to call the shots of all his political games and return as the winner time after time, including a third term that started in 2017 and is still ongoing. [1] As a result, in the course of ten years he built a massive party machine that has come to dominate the Bulgarian political system, where electoral volatility is quite high and party discipline a rare phenomenon.

This political context makes Borissov's survival in PM office an even more interesting case. Our article will use insights from the literature on new parties in government, executive power in post-communist Europe as well as the literature on prime-ministerial survival and coalition theory to examine Borissov I (2009–2013), Borissov II (2014–2016), and the early years of Borissov III (2017–2019). Using secondary sources, we will demonstrate how Borissov succeeded to maintain the chief executive office by looking at two main dimensions: his relationship with other parties inside and outside the parliament as well as the mechanisms of cabinet management. [2]

Challenges of PM survival in the CEE context

There are several theoretical considerations regarding the ability of PM Borissov, as chair of a new party in a post-communist context, to maintain a stable position vis-à-vis the parliamentary setting and other institutions in the political system.

PMs accessing the chief executive office from within new parties experience specific challenges presented by the newness of the party they represent. Parties that enter the electoral process for the first time can be either genuinely new or splinters from existing ones. Of particular relevance are the genuinely new parties (GNPs) defined as "parties that are not successors to any previous parliamentary parties, have a novel name and structure, and do not have any important figures from past democratic politics among their major members" (Sikk 2005, 399). Such GNPs are inexperienced in dealing with internal developments such as leadership changes, ideological fluidity, and organisational problems (Deschouwer 2008, 2). All these dimensions make them face, if they come into power, specific challenges of governing.

PMs who come from such parties share these challenges. GNPs embarking on a governing tenure tend to experience challenges to their leadership, identity, and vote base (Deschouwer 2008, 4). Most fundamentally, when gaining enough parliamentary seats to be in cabinet, they come to replace their vote-seeking ambitions with office-seeking ones (Buelens and Hino 2008, 157–175). Such a change impacts and challenges the party in all its functions. A GNP participating in government needs to fill political offices – and faces particular challenges in doing this.

To begin with, it needs to find enough suitable and reliable appointees to support it in various offices of the state. GNPs might experience difficulties in recruiting such people in large enough numbers. In addition, the distribution of offices might lead to elite conflicts, further destabilising the party (Deschouwer 2008, 4–5; Bolleyer 2008, 32–33). Further, in transitioning from the parliamentary opposition or from an extra-parliamentary protest position to a governing party, the GNP undergoes significant identity change. It will need to compromise to maintain its position – whether governing alone or in coalition

– and this will certainly lead to vote loss particularly as incumbency begins to weigh in (Bolleyer 2008, 30–31).

In addition, the survival of PMs as "primus inter pares" reflects the ability of the cabinet as such to remain in office. Consequently, cabinet duration is affected by various conditions (Müller, Bergman, and Ilonszki 2019). Structural attributes of the cabinet itself such as its majority status or the ideologically compatibility of coalition partners can prolong its life while the opposite will shorten its tenure (Müller, Bergman, and Ilonszki 2019, 17–18). Institutional conditions will further constrain the chances of a cabinet to remain in power: the presence of investiture vote might lengthen it, while strong and unified opposition might shorten it (Laver and Schofield 1990, 147–158). Last, critical events, such as death of a leader, war involvement, and economic crises but also civil protests and natural disasters, can be the "force" that brings party governments down (Browne, Frendreis, and Gleiber 1984, 179).

The ability of PMs in CEE to survive in office is also impacted by the specific realities of the post-communist context. As Blondel and Müller-Rommel (2001, 10–12) and Grotz and Weber (2012) have argued, both external tensions – such as institutional demarcation between government and opposition – and internal tensions – such as the politicisation of the bureaucracy and the heritage of the communist patronage system – create a particularly challenging situation. Unpredictability, inefficiently and increased dependence on the dynamics of the (unstable) party system have characterised post-communist governments (Grotz and Weber 2012; Blondel and Müller-Rommel 2001, 13). In such less predictable environment (Baylis 2007), the specific features of the PM and their relationships with the other parties, and institutional set-up come to play an extremely important role for the longevity of the PM (Grotz and Kukec in this issue). Support by their own party is fundamental to PMs in post-electoral situations, while the presence of a strong president is often detrimental to the ability of PM's to remain in power long.

In addition to these structural features that are likely to impact the longevity of a PM, there are also several individual factors that, research has shown, make for more or less durable political leaders (Dowding 2013). Literature on the leadership capital index, for example, distinguishes between political capital and leadership capital and argue that this is the latter, composed of individual skills, relations and reputation that provides a useful analytical tool to study political leadership comparatively (Bennister et al. 2015, 434). This index they come up to measure leadership capital has been used to assess the strength of numerous executive leaders and explain certain patterns of executive durability (such as Helms 2016 on German chancellors and Burrett 2016 on Japanese PMs). For the present purposes, we focus on the more structural determinants of the durability of prime ministers, while arguably some of the discussion also touched upon the personal style of PM Borissov and the interplay of these individual and structural characteristics.[3] Abilit

Theoretically, a PM coming to power for the first time, from within a new party, with a minority cabinet, within a somewhat under-institutionalised party system and a fluid institutional setting, would be faced with a tough job to maintain her cabinet and herself in power. Such situations, we argue, are likely to put an even greater burden on these men and women because of the unpredictability and instability of political behaviour within post-communist political systems. PMs within such situations are likely to keep shorter reigns on their cabinets, and remain, even more than in ordinary situations, the focal points for dealing with the challenges of governing such as appointing people to public office, maintaining the links to their vote base and securing internal party stability.

Within the context of these expected challenges, Boyko Borissov was unlikely to succeed in maintaining cabinet stability and surviving in power. Leader of a GNP, heading a minority cabinet and faced with heterogeneous opposition and unpredictable party support in parliament (Grotz and Weber 2016, 452), he should have had a short tenure in chief executive office and disappeared into political irrelevance, just as his political mentor Saxecoburggotski did. Borissov was the first PM since Dimitrov in 1991 to be faced with a minority situation in parliament. His second cabinet was even a more interesting case as it was composed of a four-party coalition that still fell short of having a majority status. Minority government entails continuous bargaining and leads to potentially lack of commitment and motivation to negotiate alternative coalitions and might lead to shorter PM durations (Somer-Topcu and Williams 2008, 317). Further, Borissov was also faced with quite ideologically diverse supporting parties, and tough situations in parliament.

In that respect, his ability to return ever more powerful to the position of the PM in 2014 and 2017 made him an unexpected game-changer in Bulgarian politics. If we use office duration as indication of political success, Borissov is clearly the most successful Bulgarian PM. As Table 1 illustrates the average prime-ministerial duration in post-communist Bulgaria is 942 days.[4] In this context, Borissov has enjoyed more than 3,043 days (as of December 31, 2019) as leader of three separate cabinets. More importantly, however, he is the only PM in the country to come back twice after his initial tenure.

The rest of this article, will analyse the behaviour of PM Borissov across his first two cabinet tenures (2009–2013 and 2014–2017) and the initial two years of his third one (2017–2019) to explore the mechanisms and strategies he used to cope with the challenges posed to him in chief executive office. We will do so along two dimensions identified as key challenges to PMs from new parties: the ability to staff governmental position with personnel, and to maintain support for their cabinets in parliament.

Borissov in the context of Bulgarian politics

The assessment of Boyko Borissov's survival as PM and the impact of his prime-ministerial tenures on Bulgarian politics requires some discussion of the context within which he emerged.

The first decade of Bulgaria's post-1989 democratic development was dominated by the successor party of the communist regime – the Bulgarian Socialist Party (BSP) – and the main opposition party – the Union of Democratic Forces (SDS). As Table 1 illustrates, the cabinets of this decade were, with one exception, composed by either of these parties and their chairmen served as PMs. In 2001, this pattern of bipolar alternation was shattered when Simeon Saxecoburggotski, the last reigning tsar (king) of Bulgaria,[5] returned to politics as party leader and head of a coalition cabinet between 2001 and 2005 (Karasimeonov 2010). As democratically appointed PM, however, he governed in what has been characterised as a Messiah role, promising to "save" the people from the oligarchy and from the eleven-year "bipolarity".[6]

Saxecoburggotski established a party, which was, as its name suggests, built around his own personality. National Movement Simeon the Second (NDSV) proclaimed a

Table 1. Prime ministers and party governments in Bulgaria (1991–2019).

Cabinet	Date in	Date out	PM duration[a]	Cabinet duration[a]	Relative duration (as proportion of possible duration)	Party composition[b]	Cabinet type[c]
Dimitrov	1991-11-08	1992-10-28	355	355	0.24	**SDS** (+DP, RDP)	MIN
Berov	1992-30-12	1994-09-08	617	617	0.57	**NI**[d], BSP, DPS	SUR
Videnov	1995-01-25	1996-12-28	703	703	0.47	**BSP**	MWC
Kostov	1997-05-21	2001-06-17	1488	1488	1.00	**SDS**, NS	SUR
Saxecoburggotski I	2001-07-24	2005-02-21	1430	1308	0.86	**NDSV**, DPS	MWC
Saxecoburggotski II	2005-02-23	2005-06-25		122	0.08	**NDSV**, DPS, NV	MWC
Stanishev	2005-16-08	2009-07-05	1419	1419	0.97	**BSP**, NDSV, DPS	SUR
Borissov I	2009-07-27	2013-02-21	1305	1305	0.87	**GERB**	MIN
Oresharski	2013-05-29	2014-07-24	419	419	0.29	**BSP**, DPS	MIN
Borissov II	2014-11-07	2016-11-14	738	738	0.49	**GERB**, RB	MIN
Borissov III	2017-05-04	current				**GERB**, UP	MWC

[a]The horizontal lines demarcate parliamentary terms. Office duration in days. Caretaker cabinets are excluded.
[b]Party of PM marked in bold; parties ordered by parliamentary size.
[c]MIN-minority; MWC-minimal winning coalition; SUR-surplus coalition.
[d]Independent PM nominated by BSP.

platform focused on economic and financial issues, while its leader repeatedly advocated the abandonment of partisanship and unification around "historical ideas and values" (Harper 2003, 336). When Saxecoburggotski assumed the post of PM, he was faced with a complete lack of organisational structures and party machine on which to draw people to his cabinet. This was clearly evident in his choice of high-level officials, in which he relied more on personal connections and friends than on party mechanisms.

One of these personnel decisions became crucial for the political development of Bulgaria. PM Saxecoburggotski appointed a somewhat unknown man, Boyko Borissov, as a Chief Secretary of the Ministry of Interior, opening up an ever growing career path for him. What brought him a massive support later was quite the opposite of the incumbent PM: his macho looks and fitting manner of talking. Borissov's eclectic image mixed several roles: firefighter, academic and personal bodyguard of the ex-communist leader Todor Zhivkov. Similarly to Saxecoburggotski, Borissov was perceived as a tough on crime savior, bringing order in the overly distorted political and social situation in the country. In 2005, as the NDSV fortunes were declining, he ran for mayor of Sofia and won the election as an independent, but with the support of NDSV. By August 2009, in his first month as PM, Borissov had a 60% approval rating, arguably the highest value for a PM in that period (Mediapool 2011).

Borissov I: a new party within a minority cabinet

How did PM Borissov deal with the challenges presented by GERB being new to the national political arena? To begin with, he pre-empted some of the typical challenges by quickly building an extensive and strong party organisation and allowing it to gain political experience by running in the European elections before joining the national political arena. Citizens for a European Development of Bulgaria (GERB) had been founded in December 2006 and built, very similarly to NDSV, around the personality of Borissov, then mayor of Sofia. GERB declared itself to be a center-right party presenting a "new rightist treaty" to the Bulgarian people based on three fundamental values: "economic freedom," "competition in an environment of clear responsibilities and rules," and "minimum state participation" (GERB 2008). In addition, the treaty advocated a strong role for the EU in guiding Bulgaria's development, and called for transparency and accountability in managing the EU funds in the country. The party quickly joined the political competition – it participated in the European elections in May 2007 and came out as the plurality winner and similarly competed and won in a lot of the local elections in October 2007. Hence, by 2009 parliamentary elections, GERB was ready to compete in the national elections. National candidate lists were composed of people with experience in local politics and the party built an extensive party organisation, which at that moment already boasted 22,000 members (Kostadinova 2017). In contrast, NDSV had about 19,000 at the very peak of its government in 2003 (Spirova 2007, 128). While these developments did not pre-empt the party from experiencing the challenges of GNPs in governing entirely, it certainly alleviated some of them.

As newcomer to the national legislative arena, GERB clearly won the 2009 elections with 38.9% of the vote and 48.7% of the seats, barely failing to get a parliament majority (Kolarova and Spirova 2010).[7] Negotiations for the future cabinet started prior to the elections, but took a different turn after them. GERB and the Blue Coalition (SK), an alliance of several center-right parties, successors of SDS that had governed the country during 1997–2001 (Kostov cabinet in Table 1), were natural allies as partners in the European Peoples' Party. The two entered into negotiations before the elections, expecting a strong performance by GERB, and for a couple of weeks, it seemed like a center-right coalition would come into government. However, once it became clear that GERB was *the* winner of the election, it decided against a coalition government. Instead, the party formed a single-party minority cabinet, asking three other parties that were on the right side of the spectrum – the Blue Coalition, the Law, Order and Justice (RZS) and Ataka – to sign an agreement promising their parliamentary support. GERB thus hoped to assume sole responsibility for a successful government policy, enjoying a comfortable majority in parliament at the same time (as the center-right parties controlled more than two thirds of the seats). While GERB offered the written agreement to the three parties, only Ataka signed it, leaving the cabinet in an official minority situation, as its actual parliamentary support continued to be mostly ad hoc.

For his cabinet, Borissov recruited mostly experts most of whom had not run for deputies in the 2009 elections and had little political experience at national level (Kolarova and Spirova 2010). This matched the promise made by GERB in the electoral campaign to break with the patronage practices of the previous governments. The number of deputy prime ministers was decreased, the controversial ministries of state administration and of emergency situations were disbanded, and various cuts in the size of the administration promised. During the second half of 2009, partly as result of this "cleaner politics" approach, the government enjoyed an increasing popularity among the Bulgarians.

Personnel policy

The troubles, however, started quickly. Between 2009 and 2012, the cabinet underwent numerous personnel changes, reflecting the difficulties faced by any new party entering national government but also the somewhat arbitrary personnel policy of Borissov. The first year in power was probably the most turbulent: during 2010, five ministers were dismissed because of public scandals, poor performance in Brussels, international embarrassment, conflict of interests, allegations of questionable economic links, inability to handle professional tasks and openly radical nationalistic statements (for details see Kolarova and Spirova 2011).

These cabinet reshuffles reflected the inability of the Borissov I cabinet to formulate efficient policy in various sectors. This was somewhat explained by the existing constrains of the poor economic situation of the country, a fiscal policy of austerity, and the international pressure coming from the EU. Choosing people whom he trusted personally rather than people with political and social connections led to a general discomfort with some of his ministerial appointments. This trend continued in the next years, although none of the personnel changes were as scandalous as the ones carried out in 2010. Ministers resigned for personal reasons, some to take on other political careers. Replacements came from the career paths within the ministries and some reflected the attempt of Borissov to look into the younger and more professional circles for ministerial appointments in high-risk policy areas. A case of point is the 38-year Diana Kovacheva, then director of Transparency International-Bulgarian Chapter who was made Minister of the Judiciary in 2011, then a key area of reform and a major issue in the EU regular monitoring reports (Kolarova and Spirova 2012).

In 2012, possibly in anticipation of the end of tenure, but also as a consequence of the continuous institutionalisation of his party, Borissov's personnel policy changed. As the party now had a six year history of elite recruitment, it had available cadres to take over the vacated cabinet positions. Party activists with limited professional and management expertise came to replace the experts with mostly corporate or professional background. The new appointees in 2012 were remarkably young for their important portfolios, but came from the active core of GERB. Their appointment was enthusiastically supported by the parliamentary group, but not by the professional circles in their respective policy areas, causing some public outcries against Borissov's choices in parliament and in the media.

Parliamentary support

In parliament, Borissov's cabinet faced weak opposition. The center-right parties – Blue Coalition (SK) and Order, Law and Justice (RZS) –, although not having signed the agreement to support the cabinet, provided the political backing needed for the PM and clearly distinguished themselves from the BSP and the party of the Turkish minority, the Movement for Rights and Freedoms (DPS), seen as the "partners in crime" at the time for having been part of the three-party coalition between 2005 and 2009.[8] A vote of no-confidence against the Borissov government was initiated by BSP and DPS on 1 October 2010, but failed as it was not supported by the rest of the opposition. In addition, the parliamentary group of GERB, although inexperienced, remained remarkably stable: unlike the ones of RZS and Ataka, which both disbanded by 2011, the GERB parliamentary group did not lose a single member. This is often attributed to the hierarchical structure instituted by Borissov within GERB and his strong leadership (Todorov 2016).

In early 2011, Borissov demonstrated his political acumen by using a seldom utilised institutional tool: a vote of confidence in the overall policy of his cabinet. With half of the opposition parties loyal to his minority cabinet, the vote passed with a comfortable margin – 141 out of the 240 MPs, with only the BSP and DPS voting against. This vote aimed to prevent the escalation of a political scandal caused by leaked wiretapped conversations between the PM and Vanyo Tanov, the National Customs Agency Director. Anticipating a vote of no-confidence that could be more problematic to manage, Borissov referred to a provision in the Rules of Organisation and Procedure of the 41st National Assembly (Art. 98) stipulating that no-confidence votes should not be initiated six months after a successful confidence vote and called the confidence vote.

The Constitutional Court declared this stipulation unconstitutional following the referral of the center-left opposition. Two more votes of no-confidence were initiated by the BSP and the DPS shortly after this decision. While both failed, in a momentous step, some of the center-right deputies from the disbanded RZS and ATAKA groups joined the center-left to show their growing dissatisfaction with PM Borissov and his cabinet, which continued into early 2013. Despite numerous policy-related challenges to the cabinet, the parliamentary opposition continued to be unable to benefit from the situation and the minority government remained in power. While Borissov's public support was declining, there was no alternative emerging in the fragmented and still publicly discredited opposition, particularly as the MPs from the smaller parties saw no chance of being re-elected. Early elections thus seemingly remained unlikely.

The surprise resignation

While in early 2013 the GERB minority government had a comfortable "working majority" of its 117 MPs and 12 independent MPs who explicitly committed themselves to support the cabinet bills, Borissov unexpectedly resigned. Major social protests had erupted against the government, first in Sofia and then in other big cities. Motivated by the high energy costs during the winter months, the protests broadened to also include environmental and anti-monopolism issues, and widened in scale and demands to call for the resignation of the finance minister and a major cabinet reshuffle. After small scale clashes with the police ensued with a few wounded protesters, PM Borissov submitted, quite unexpectedly, the resignation of the government on 20 February 2013. Most observers agree that Borissov shrewdly decided to distance himself from the executive. Following constitutional provisions, a different, caretaker, cabinet is appointed in Bulgaria and the parliament disbanded if early elections are called at any moment. The President thus disbanded parliament and appointed a non-partisan cabinet headed by Marin Raykov. Borissov thus let the caretaker PM lead the country into early elections in March 2013, instead of waiting out until the regularly scheduled ones three month later (Kolarova and Spirova 2015). At that point Borissov had almost finished his mandate: the resignation came when already 87% of his constitutional mandate were passed (see Table 1 for comparative indicators). As parliament had not requested his resignation, the image of him calling the shots was maintained. As a result, at the early elections in March 2013, GERB maintained its plurality position in electoral competition. Still, GERB's loss of about 20 deputies and the presence of only four parties in parliament allowed the second-placed BSP to form a center-left coalition. A period of political instability followed, ending with another call for early elections in 2014 (Kolarova and Spirova 2015; Spirova and Sharenkova-Toshkova 2019).

Borissov II: battling ideological heterogeneity

Only 18 months after the February 2013 protests that led to his withdrawal from power, Borissov re-emerged from the 2014 election as the leader of the country's most popular party again, and this time without any alternatives for taking over the PM position. However, there was a total of eight parties and electoral alliances gaining seats in parliament and executive coalition negotiations did not promise to be easy. After a prolonged process, GERB formed a coalition with the Reformers' Block (RB), an alliance of several parties, and asked for the parliamentary support of two smaller parties: the Alternative for the Revival of Bulgaria (ABV), formed in the early 2014 as a splinter from the BSP around Bulgaria's former president Parvanov, and the Patriotic Front (PF), an alliance of two nationalist parties.

This coalition controlled 45% of the seats in parliament, but had the promised support of another 30 deputies, a total of about 57% of the seats. Borissov's second cabinet took office on 7 November, promising in its program a "stable parliamentary majority and a pro-European reformist government for the stable development of Bulgaria" (Ministerski savet 2014). Only GERB and RB formally signed the coalition agreement; ABV agreed to support the government in exchange for one ministerial portfolio for ABV, but was not formally part of the coalition agreement, and PF exchanged its support for policy concessions, including the consideration of proposals to end broadcast news in Turkish on Bulgarian National TV. The coalition was hailed as the cabinet of a "reformers' majority," but was so diverse that maintaining it required strong political will and acumen. While GERB was not a new party any more, it was still faced with some of the challenges that characterised Borissov's first cabinet.

Personnel policy and parliamentary support

Early personnel changes in Borissov's second cabinet reflected the style of his first one: the PM took decisions based on his personal approval or disapproval of developments in the ministries and agencies. However, while Borissov could control his own party and its elite, the instability of his coalition partners became evident as policy disagreements and conflicts emerged. In fact, cabinet reshuffles and intra-coalitional dynamics became intimately intertwined.

One case of ministerial replacement is indicative of the challenges the heterogeneous coalition was posing for the PM. In May 2015, Minister of the Judiciary Hristo Ivanov (RB) sought to increase the independence of the judiciary and limit its politicisation. This necessitated constitutional changes and a bill to that effect was introduced in the National Assembly. While publicly hailed as the first real attempt to reform the judiciary sector by professional organisations and civil society groups, the bill proved very difficult politically. In the parliamentary vote in early December, the two-thirds majority required for constitutional amendments failed to materialise, thus de facto refusing to support the minister on that key issue, leading to his resignation. Clearly an indication of growing intra-coalitional problems, PM Borissov took the opportunity created by the inability of the junior coalition partner to nominate a replacement from the ranks of GERB. The parliamentary vote for the new cabinet minister indicated both further intra-coalition trouble as half of the RB deputies votes against the GERB candidate Bachvarova, but also a diversification of the support for the cabinet, as the oppositional Bulgarian Democratic Centre (BDC) backed the new appointment. The choice of a GERB candidate was thus a clear warning signal to the governing partners and the opposition that dynamics within the coalition were changing, and Borissov used the vote as an opportunity to clarify his friends and foes within the parliamentary arena. The move demonstrated the maneuvering necessary to maintain a heterogeneous coalition in an even more heterogeneous parliament.

These tensions only increased over the course of 2016, when further personnel changes in the cabinet indicated problems within the Reformists Bloc. In March, Democrats for Strong Bulgaria (DSB), a constituent party of RB openly joined the opposition. In May, in anticipation of the presidential elections scheduled for November, the left-wing coalition partner ABV left the government, and its minister Ivaylo Kalfin (Minister of Labour and Social Policy) resigned and was replaced by the independent Zornitsa Russinova. This was seen as the first definite sign that the coalition formula of the cabinet needed to change. In fact, it led to renegotiations to incorporate cabinet ministers from the Patriotic Front, which until then had not been part of the cabinet. Cabinet reshuffling was planned for after the presidential elections, and political observers expected that the share of RB ministerial portfolios would be decreased to reflect RB's decreasing support for the cabinet in parliamentary votes and its anticipated poor performance at the presidential elections.

The unnecessary resignation

At that moment, Borissov seemed to have decided to capitalise on the growing problems within and among his partners. The popularity of his cabinet and himself was declining substantially as the year went on (Alpha Research 2016), with the intra-coalition tensions and scandals seen as the major reason for this development. As the presidential elections approached, he made a clear public commitment to step down as PM if the GERB presidential candidate failed to win. The landslide victory of the candidate backed by the Socialists in the second round of the presidential race indicated that a considerable proportion of government supporters voted for the opposition candidate. True to his promise, Borissov resigned on 14 November. This step was not necessary in political terms, as the cabinet relied on the support of more than 140 MPs (with 121 needed for a majority). Over the course of the year, parliamentary life had reflected the gradual change in the coalition format, but a vote of no-confidence would not have received the necessary support. Parliamentary party groups remained fairly stable with the exception of DPS, which lost quite a few members due to internal conflicts. With a visible stronger link between the two nationalistic parties – Patriotic Front and ATAKA, with the latter moving from a radical opposition to a support party –, the situation in parliament could have allowed Borissov to remain in power. But he clearly had other plans. In fact, as it transpired in the weeks after, when the other parliamentary factions were trying to form a new cabinet, Borissov was determined to push for early elections. With GERB refusing to participate in the cabinet talks, the newly elected president Radev dissolved parliament and called early elections.

Borissov III: two years of a streamlined coalition

It did not surprise many observers that the elections of 25 March 2017 saw GERB emerging as the dominant party for the fourth time in a row since 2009. As Figure 1 illustrates

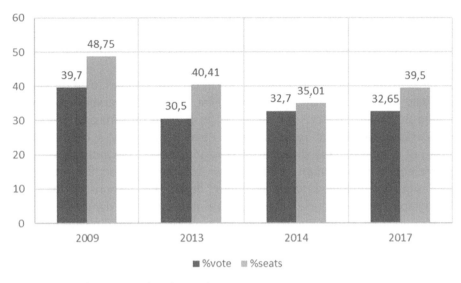

Figure 1. GERB performance in legislative elections 2009–2017.

the party managed to increase its seat share and re-assume a much more central role in the coalition government that did not have a minority status any more.

With GERB being clearly the strongest party in parliament, Borissov was set to remain PM. With the nationalist United Patriots (UP) as coalition partner, Borissov announced the agreement on the government program on 13 April 2017 and was voted into office on 4 May 2017 by parliament.

This cabinet was a less diverse and more right-of-center version of Borissov II, as two of the more mainstream, but also ideologically heterogeneous partners – Reformist Block (RB) and Alternative for Bulgarian Revival (ABV) – had gone. Although the new cabinet posed less challenges in terms of ideological cohesiveness, the problems of allying with the nationalist UP were demonstrated immediately. By then, of course, GERB was no longer a new party and a lot of its original challenges had transformed to reflect intra-coalition dynamics rather problems of fledgling executive party.

Personnel policy

The personnel policy of Borissov III indicated this shift. Only days after his appointment, the Deputy Minister of Regional Development and Public Works, Pavel Tenev (UP), resigned after a scandal broke out because an old photograph appeared in Internet of him giving a Hitler salute to wax figures of Nazi officers in a museum in Paris. Similarly, the appointment of UP co-chairman and Deputy Prime Minister Valeri Simeonov to head Bulgaria's National Council on Co-operation on Ethnic and Integration Issues prompted protests among NGOs. Allegations of corrupt deals brought the Minister of Health down in early October, when Borissov replaced him with another GERB nominee. Further personnel changes followed in 2018, and reflected both response to policy problems and intra-coalitional conflicts.

In September 2018, a tragic bus accident on the Sofia-Svoge road led to the resignation of three cabinet members: the Minister of Interior, the Minister of Regional

Development and Public Works and the Minister of Transport, Information Technology and Communications. Their resignation occurred within a week of the accident, for which poor road reconstruction and inefficient control and maintenance appeared to be to blame. As all three ministers were from the GERB quota, the party suffered a serious blow in terms of public criticism (Kolarova and Spirova 2019). In November, two scandals triggered further resignations. First, in early November, accusations of exchanging Bulgarian passports for bribes led to a wave of dismissals in the Agency for Bulgarians Abroad, including its chairman Petar Haralampiev, a UP representative. Although not a minister, the dismissal of Haralampiev and his indictment for taking bribes challenged the position of the junior coalition partner. Later that month, another resignation followed. Valeri Simeonov, deputy PM responsible for economic and demographic policy, resigned after 26 days of public protests demanding his dismissal. These protests were triggered by Simeonov's inappropriate and offensive comments concerning the parents of disabled children who had been acting, for more than 240 days, as a pressure group in demand of additional social services and financing for their children (Kolarova and Spirova 2019). Borissov's grip on power was thus somewhat challenged as both ministers from the coalition partner, but also some personally chosen by him began to attract public outcry.

Parliamentary support

Despite these scandals and public allegations of misconduct, Borissov and his third cabinet survived three parliamentary votes of no confidence. In addition to maintaining the integrity of his own parliamentary group, Borissov also preserved the firm backing of his coalition partners. All three non-confidence votes were introduced by the Socialists and supported by the DPS, but none managed to attract enough deputies from the governing majority or its tacit supporter Volya.[9] Indeed, the voting patterns in all three no-confidence motions, as well as the general voting pattern in the National Assembly, point to the new supporting party role played by Volya. This leads to a widened parliamentary support for the cabinet, despite the active opposition by BSP and DPS.

Conclusion

As of the end of 2019, PM Borissov had by far outdone the Bulgarian PMs before him to survive in chief executive office. None of his counterparts since 1990 has managed to return to the PM position and most lost major political influence even within their own parties. Even Borissov's political "father" Simeon Saxecoburggotski was much less successful. His popularity deteriorated dramatically during just one prime-ministerial tenure, his party remained in power but sentenced itself to political suicide by joining the triple coalition of 2005 and by 2009, and finally disappeared from any meaningful position in Bulgarian politics while Saxecoburggotski returned to his royal position as political observer.

What can explain Borissov's extraordinary longevity in chief executive office in the Bulgarian context? What does the experiences of Borissov I, II and III suggest in terms of the theoretical considerations about PMs from a genuinely new party and faced with a minority situation in cabinet and unstable political allies suggested in the beginning of this article? In many ways, the longevity of Borissov contradicts the theoretical expectations which suggest a short, unstable tenure in office.

First of all, to pre-empt some of the challenges facing new parties in government, Borissov moved fast to build GERB as a viable political entity. Political activity started at the local level, and GERB invested quickly into setting up a strong organisational network and a pool of local political elites. This helped in a significant way with the recruitment of cadres for the executive and securing support from the party on the ground for the newly minted PM and his minority cabinet during 2009–2013. This suggests that the newness of parties as hindrance to PM durability needs to be seen in context, as sometimes developments on sub-national level might be concealed by the newness at the national political scene while at the same time they might prove crucial for the ability of the party (and its PM) to govern.

In a similar vein, to resolve the problem of not having enough reliable party representatives to staff the executive, Borissov built a loyal personal following. Unlike Saxecoburggotski, he intertwined it within the organisational structure of the party he chaired. As a result, he was able to maintain a strong supply of GERB appointees in various levels of the state administration, including local government. This tendency, naturally, created problems among the public and his political partners. Personnel decisions within the executive made with such considerations in mind, often, especially during his first cabinet, left aside concerns with professionalism and expertise. This trend was both a blessing and a curse for Borissov's ability to remain in the driver's seat of Bulgarian politics. Accusations of lack of concern with the opinion of the partners were expressed publicly in the media by coalition co-chair Simeonov in 2017, causing further tremors in the political alliance. This suggests a tradeoff between a leader individual ability to build a following and their party ability to maintain stable support by its partners. In turn, this points to the need to consider individual and structural determinants of PM power in an interactive manner, offering further empirical evidence to approaches such as Strangio et al. (2013) in understanding and explaining executive power.

A third feature that has contributed to Borissov's almost permanent place in politics seems to be an uncanny ability to bluff his way into a more powerful position by using the existing institutional possibilities. In both 2013 and 2016, he resigned when he did not have to, making these decisions an issue of personal honour. As a result, he was able, in one case, to distance himself and his party from the incumbency and not experience all negative associated with it, and in the second case, managed to shake off inconvenient coalition partners and return to power in a much more trimmed down and homogenous cabinet. These decisions were not without political risk, but in situations where alternatives were almost non-existent, his decisions seemed to have brought only benefits to him and GERB. By distancing himself from the incumbency in both cases, he managed to capitalise on the traditional support of his party. It also demonstrated a somewhat pragmatic approach to politics – Borissov and GERB have forged coalitions with center-left and center-right parties that would allow him to remain in the chief executive office.

These decisions helped Borissov pre-empt another challenge that new parties face in government – that of their identity changing from a challenger to a member of the establishment. Going beyond the particular case, this again demonstrates that there are

48 PRIME MINISTERS AND PARTY GOVERNMENTS IN CENTRAL AND EASTERN EUROPE

institutional opportunities that can be used by new parties to bypass their obvious short-comings and capitalise on their images as challengers, even when in government. To take this further, this can lead to an alternative theoretical proposition: the newness of the party brings with itself an energising political momentum that allows such parties to distance themselves from incumbency with greater success than established parties.

Despite his ups and down, Borissov remained the most popular politician in the country with approval ratings have remained stable at about 33% through the ups and down of his political decade (Alpha Research 2019). His experience shows that the challenges facing new parties in government and their leaders as PMs can be partially countered by targeted personnel policy and smart choice of allies in coalition negotiations. While history is still to show how Borissov will exit the political arena and whether he will not be outmaneuvered by his competitors, his political figure will certainly leave a mark on Bulgarian politics and coalition governance. Further research into the interplay of personalities and party governments in the CEE region is clearly needed to understand why some PMs from new parties make it and others do not, even when faced by similar institutional contexts. Such insights will certainly contribute to the more general understanding of PM survival and the study of coalition politics more generally.

Notes

1. This article does not assess or explain the success of PM Borissov in terms of the policy impact or the general development of the country under his cabinets, but only his ability to remain in power and return to power from 2009 until 2019.
2. Parts of the data and discussion used here have been published in Kolarova and Spirova 2010, 2011, 2012, 2017 and 2019 and Spirova 2015.
3. In fact, the index itself combines both some of the explanatory variables (relations within the party, leadership position) and the dependent variable (time in office) of this study. While we do not use the index, we use the equivalents of some of its components (Bennister et al. 2015, 424) to explore the relationship among them.
4. Because of the more complicated constitutional mandate, the cabinets of the Grant National Assembly (1990-1991) are excluded from the analysis.
5. His supporters as well as his self-presentation still refers to him as His Majesty Simeon II, but for the rest, he remains Simeon Saxecoburggotski, Bulgarian citizen and political leader. Simeon II never abdicated from the throne which he was forced to leave as a six-year-old child and then reside in Spain in exile until 2001 (Kalinova and Baeva 2010).
6. On 6 April 2001, two and a half months before the regularly scheduled elections, Simeon Saxecoburggotski delivered a notorious speech in Sofia in which he made big promises, the boldest of which was to change Bulgaria in 800 days (Simeon II 2001).
7. The Bulgarians Socialist Party (BSP), the second largest in parliament, had 16.7% of the seats.
8. The 2005–2009 coalition of BSP, DPS and NDSV had been a coalition of mutual accommodation that guaranteed the distribution of benefits to all members, a practice strongly disliked by the public.
9. Volya, a small party that joined the National Assembly in 2017, is insofar similar to GERB as it is built around the personality of its leader, the businessman Veselin Mareshki (Spirova 2018, 39).

Disclosure statement

No potential conflict of interest was reported by the author(s).

References

Alpha Research. 2019. Оценка за дейността на министър председателя. [Assessment of the work of the PM], https://alpharesearch.bg/monitoring/26/.

Alpha Research. Оценка за дейността на правителството [Assessment of the work of the cabinet], http://alpharesearch.bg/bg/socialni_izsledvania/political_and_economic_monitoring/pravitelstvo.html.

Baylis, T. A. 2007. "Embattled Executives: Prime Ministerial Weakness in East Central Europe." *Communist and Post-Communist Studies* 40 (1): 81–106.

Bennister, M., P. 't Hart, and B. Worthy. 2015. "Assessing the Authority of Political Office-Holders: The Leadership Capital Index." *West European Politics* 38 (3): 417–440.

Blondel, J., and F. Müller-Rommel, eds. 2001. *Cabinets in Eastern Europe*. London: Palgrave.

Bolleyer, N. 2008. "The Organizational Costs of Public Office." In *New Parties in Government. In Power for the First Time*, edited by K. Deschouwer, 17–44. London: Routledge.

Browne, E. C., J. P. Frendreis, and D. W. Gleiber. 1984. "An 'Events' Approach to the Problem of Cabinet Stability." *Comparative Political Studies* 17 (2): 167–197.

Buelens, J., and A. Hino. 2008. "The Electoral Fate of New Parties in Government." In *New Parties in Government. In Power for the First Time*, edited by K. Deschouwer, 177–194. London: Routledge.

Burrett, T. 2016. "Explaining Japan's Revolving Door Premiership: Applying the Leadership Capital Index." *Politics and Governance* 4 (2): 36–53. doi:10.17645/pag.v4i2.575.

Deschouwer, Kris. 2008. *New Parties in Government. In Power for the First Time*. London: Routledge.

Dowding, K. 2013. "Prime-Ministerial Power Institutional and Personal Factors." In *Understanding Prime-Ministerial Performance: Comparative Perspectives*, edited by Paul Strangio, Paul 't Hart, and James Walter, 57–78. Oxford. Scholarship Online: May 2013, DOI:10.1093/acprof:oso/9780199666423.003.0001

GERB. 2008. The New Rightist Treaty for Bulgaria. Available at: http://gerb-bg.com/Gerb_Program_final_eng.doc Last accessed on April 15, 2008.

Grotz, F., and T. Weber. 2012. "Party Systems and Government Stability in Central and Eastern Europe." *World Politics* 64 (4): 699–740.

Grotz, F., and T. Weber. 2016. "New Parties, Information Uncertainty, and Government Formation: Evidence from Central and Eastern Europe." *European Political Science Review* 8 (3): 449–472.

Grotz, F., and T. Weber. 2017. "Prime Ministerial Tenure in Central and Eastern Europe: The Role of Party Leadership and Cabinet Experience." In *Parties, Governments and Elites: The Comparative Study of Democracy*, edited by P. Harfst, I. Kubbe, and T. Poguntke, 229–248. Wiesbaden: Springer.

Harper, M. A. G. 2003. "The 2001 Parliamentary and Presidential Elections in Bulgaria." *Electoral Studies* 22 (2): 325–395.

Helms, L. 2016. "The Politics of Leadership Capital in Compound Democracies: Inferences from the German Case." *European Political Science Review* 8 (2): 285–310. doi:10.1017/S1755773915000016.

Kalinova, E., and I. Baeva. 2010. *Bulgarian Transitions 1939-2005*. Sofia: Paradigma.

Karasimeonov, G. 2010. *The Party System in Bulgaria*. Sofia: Friedrich Ebert Stiftung.

Kolarova, R., and M. Spirova. 2010. "Bulgaria 2009." *European Journal of Political Research Political Data Yearbook* 49 (7-8): 909–918.

Kolarova, R., and M. Spirova. 2011. "Bulgaria 2010." *European Journal of Political Research Political Data Yearbook* 50 (7-8): 49–56.

Kolarova, R., and M. Spirova. 2012. "Bulgaria 2012." *European Journal of Political Research Political Data Yearbook* 51 (1): 922–927.

Kolarova, R., and M. Spirova. 2015. "Bulgaria 2013." *European Journal of Political Research Political Data Yearbook* 53 (1): 45–56.

Kolarova, R., and M. Spirova. 2017. "Bulgaria 2016." *European Journal of Political Research Political Data Yearbook* 56 (1): 36–43.

Kolarova, R., and M. Spirova. 2019. "Bulgaria: Political Developments and Data in 2018." *European Journal of Political Research Political Data Yearbook* 58 (1): 37–42.

Kostadinova, T., et al. 2017. "Bulgaria: Organizational Structure and Trends in Bulgarian Party Politics." In *Organizational Structures of Political Parties in Central and Eastern European Countries*, edited by K. Sobolewska-Myślik, 85–108. Krakow: Jagiellonian University Press.

Laver, M., and N. Schofield. 1990. *Multiparty Government: The Politics of Coalition in Europe*. Oxford: Oxford University Press.

Mediapool. 2011. https://www.mediapool.bg/mbmd-s-nai-dobar-rezultat-e-kabinetat-na-kostov-s-nai-visoko-doverie-e-premierat-borisov-news187631.html.

Ministerski savet. 2014. *Programna deklaracija*. Available at: http://www.government.bg/cgi-bin/e-cms/vis/vis.pl?s=001&p=0211&n=122&g, last accessed 15 February 2015.

Mueller-Rommel, F. 2005. *Types of Cabinet Durability in Central Eastern Europe*. UC Irvine: Center for the Study of Democracy. Retrieved from https://escholarship.org/uc/item/8cv4134w.

Müller, W. C., T. Bergman, and G. Ilonszki. 2019. "Extending the Coalition Life-Cycle Approach to Central Eastern Europe – An Introduction." In *Coalition Governance in Central Eastern Europe*, edited by T. Bergman, G. Ilonszki, and W. C. Müller, 1–59. Oxford: Oxford University Press.

Sikk, A. 2005. "How Unstable? Volatility and the Genuinely New Parties in Eastern Europe." *European Journal of Political Research* 44 (3): 391–412.

Simeon, I. I. 2001. "Обръщение към нацията." *Mediapool.bg*, April 1. https://www.mediapool.bg/obrashtenie-kam-naroda-na-simeon-sakskoburggotski-6-april-2001-news15818.html.

Somer-Topcu, Z., and L. K. Williams. 2008. "Survival of the Fittest? Cabinet Duration in Postcommunist Europe." *Comparative Politics* 40 (3): 313–329.

Spirova, M. 2007. *Political Parties in Post-Communist Systems: Formation, Persistence, and Change*. New York: Palgrave Macmillan.

Spirova, M. 2015. "Bulgaria." *European Journal of Political Research Political Data Yearbook* 54 (1): 44–53.

Spirova, M., and R. Sharenkova-Toshkova. 2019. "Bulgaria Since 1989." In *Central and Southeast European Politics Since 1989*, edited by S. P. Ramet, and C. M. Hassenstab, 449–476. Cambridge: Cambridge University Press.

Strangio, P., P. 't Hart, and J. Walter. 2013. "Prime Ministers and the Performance of Public Leadership." In *Understanding Prime-Ministerial Performance: Comparative Perspectives*, edited by Paul Strangio, Paul 't Hart, and James Walter, 1–31. Oxford: Oxford University Press. Oxford Scholarship Online: May 2013, DOI:10.1093/acprof:oso/9780199666423.003.0001

Todorov, A. 2016. *Политическата хегемония на ГЕРБ* [The political hegemony of GERB] http://eprints.nbu.bg/3430/1/%D0%9F%D0%BE%D0%BB%D0%B8%D1%82%D0%B8%D1%87%D0%B5%D1%81%D0%BA%D0%B0%D1%82%D0%B0%20%D1%85%D0%B5%D0%B3%D0%B5%D0%BC%D0%BE%D0%BD%D0%B8%D1%8F%20%D0%BD%D0%B0%20%D0%93%D0%95%D0%A0%D0%91.pdf.

∂ OPEN ACCESS

Prime ministers in minority governments: the case of Hungary

Daniel Kovarek ⓘ

ABSTRACT
Whereas early scholarship depicted minority cabinets as weak recent findings demonstrate how various factors contribute to effective minority governance. Nevertheless, the role of prime ministers (PMs) was largely ignored in the performance of these cabinets. The paper addresses this problem by comparing Hungary's only two minority governments in an MSSD framework. Combining a qualitative review with a quantitative analysis of voting patterns in Parliament, it argues that differences in aforementioned cabinets' policy performance can be traced back to contrasting ideological position of PMs and subsequent ideological moderation. These findings have important implications for minority governments in majoritarian and polarised contexts.

Introduction

Throughout Central and Eastern Europe (CEE), cabinets tend to be relatively short-lived and showcase high rates of premature termination compared to their Western counterparts (Grotz and Weber 2012; Savage 2013). Nevertheless, when it comes to institutional stability, Hungary stands out as the region's pre-eminent country. No snap elections have ever been called and except for three, all PMs have assumed their office after regular elections. This has invited scholars to examine structural and contextual factors enabling the extraordinary stability of governments – at least by CEE standards – in Hungary: a frozen party system, the constructive vote of no-confidence, entrenched bipolar competition and high levels of ideological polarisation (Vegetti 2019). At the same time, "counterfactuals ", i.e. the single two instances of minority cabinets in Hungary were inevitably pushed to the blind spot of comparative research.

This study addresses this gap by scrutinising these two minority governments, led by Ferenc Gyurcsány and Gordon Bajnai, respectively. They provide an excellent opportunity for comparison under a MSSD framework: both cabinets were single-party ones, formally supported only by the Socialists (MSZP) and largely relying on liberal (SZDSZ) MPs when passing legislation. Despite other similar factors, such as the share of expert ministers, governments' (negative) agenda-setting powers or party concentration, the assessment of these two cabinets' *policy performance* varies considerably.

This is an Open Access article distributed under the terms of the Creative Commons Attribution License (http://creativecommons.org/licenses/by/4.0/), which permits unrestricted use, distribution, and reproduction in any medium, provided the original work is properly cited.

I argue that this difference can be traced back to the PMs' contrasting ideological position – and subsequently the divergent strategies pursued when securing legislative backing for government initiatives. The paper demonstrates how Bajnai shifted his cabinet's image towards the ideological centre by offering various policy concessions and endorsing symbolic issues traditionally owned by right-wing parties, which facilitated obtaining the votes of SZDSZ and MDF MPs. In contrast, Gyurcsány's progressive self-positioning and leftist reform policies made it harder for other parties to externally support his minority cabinet.

According to existing scholarship, minority cabinet performance is linked to factors such as ideological proximity, location in ideological space, multilevel dynamics, bloc politics or alternative majorities (Green-Pedersen 2001; Green-Pedersen and Thomsen 2005; Field 2009; Klüver and Zubek 2018). Nonetheless, the PMs' role in any of these mechanisms remains unexplored and invites for further empirical scrutiny. Case selection in this article rules out most aforementioned factors and addresses the gap in the literature by studying minority governments in CEE. Such cabinets occur relatively frequently in the region, but remain distinct from their well-studied Scandinavian and Western European counterparts, as polarisation and cleavages over communist successor parties potentially impedes harnessing external support from the another side of the aisle.

Despite their short tenure, the cases explored in this paper are not caretaker cabinets, but rather instances of minority party governments managing financial crises and governing through serious economic hardships. Solving such crises requires not only quick executive action and comprehensive reform policies, but also the support of the majority of legislators. Understanding *how* the latter is obtained by minority cabinets that undertake more than running the administration while completing their tenure should be of elevated concern for future scholarship.

The remainder of the article is organised as follows. The second section reviews institutional factors, hypothesised by existing literature to enable effective minority governance. The next section discusses the case selection. The fourth section contrasts the political career of Gyurcsány and Bajnai. The next section offers a qualitative analysis of their ideological and economic position, whereas the penultimate section performs an empirical analysis of minority cabinets' policy performance. The last section concludes, elaborates on the generalisability of findings and showcase avenues for future research.

Minority cabinets and policy performance

Minority cabinets are not necessarily weak: they might perform well and govern effectively (Green-Pedersen 2001; Field 2009). Klüver and Zubek (2018) have tested two related hypotheses: one derived from the so-called *positional agenda power* theory and another emphasising the importance of *ideological proximity*. The former claims that minority cabinets' performance is a function of their location in the centre of the ideological space, whereas the latter posits the essential role of the closeness of opposition parties to the government. For Sweden and Denmark, the authors demonstrate that ideological distance between government and opposition diminishes legislative reliability, while they find no empirical evidence for the relationship between minority cabinets' median position in the policy space and their effectiveness.

Minority governments might also *exploit multilevel dynamics*: relying on regional parties, they can obtain their external support in the federal legislature in exchange for providing sub-national support for them (Field 2009). Other studies emphasise the relevance of "alternative majorities" and "patchwork agreements" for well-performing minority governments (Green-Pedersen 2001). If these were absent, minority cabinets in Denmark could only showcase a limited governing capacity, as their presence has allowed opposition parties to seek (and obtain) policy influence without losing their political profile.

Bloc politics is also linked to effective minority governments (Green-Pedersen and Thomsen 2005). When governments cannot rely on a bloc of exclusively left- or right-wing parties for passing legislation, legislatures and cabinets are characterised by political stalemate and ineffectiveness, respectively. Contrarily, having a bloc majority splits the opposition, and incentivises at least some of the MPs to influence policy, securing government stability. Furthermore, polarisation may seriously hinder minority governments from building winning coalitions around their legislative agenda, as a certain degree of consensus across left-wing and right-wing blocs is essential for effective governance (Green-Pedersen 2001; Green-Pedersen and Thomsen 2005).

In contrast to the mentioned attributes of parties and party systems, scholarship on PMs' role in minority governments is limited. As minority cabinets are installed, executive–legislative relations change (Lundberg 2013), but we have yet to learn more about the role of PMs without parliamentary majorities in policymaking. Some scrutinise PMs' preference for selecting expert or partisan ministers, aiming to reinforce cabinet stability or to negotiate policy with opposition parties, respectively (Alexiadou 2015; Teruel and Mir 2018). Australia has seen some independent MPs lending external support to the Gillard cabinet primarily because of their confidence in the PM and her personal abilities (Kefford and Weeks 2018, 9). Similarly, PMs heading minority governments in Canada promoted policies of a wide ideological range as "tactical manoeuvering", securing a majority by "utilising policy moderation"; one of them even used minority government years to push the Conservatives ideologically towards the median voter (Cody 2008, 31–33). Anecdotal evidence aside, there is little work on how PMs' ideological position influences cabinet dynamics.

What role does the PMs' ideological position have an effective policy performance of minority governments? How can PMs signal their cabinets' centrist spatial position in the absence of a bipolar opposition and coalition parties' median position? I address these questions by analysing two cases from Hungary, where PMs are relatively strong, but institutional arrangements make effective policy performance of minority governments unlikely.

I define a government's policy performance as a function of being able to pass major legal changes, to implement important reforms concerning several policy areas and, in general, of its legislative output. This could be operationalised as a higher share of passed bills or enacting more lasting and more effective policies, as judged by experts.

Note that while I do not treat the diverse partisan composition of legislative majorities alone as an indicator of successful policy performance (i.e. cabinets are not performing better if bills are passed with the support of an ideologically heterogeneous coalition), for Hungary's single-party minority cabinets, this is a necessary requirement for securing legislative backing for their proposals. It is also worth mentioning that (Helms 2020, 657) "legislative output, or the amount of major reform bills, of a government" is not strongly correlated with public approval (or expert evaluation) of cabinets' performance, although this paper will make every effort to compare these two governments alongside the latter dimension as well.

By conceptualising performance in terms of policy success, I aim to present an approach well-suited for comparing cabinets, as established conceptualisations (Helms 2020, 657) – e.g. coalition stability, subsequent alternation or duration – offer little help when such variables are held constant for both cases presented in this study. Furthermore, examining patterns of legislative support for government-introduced bills and (successful or failed) realisation of reform policies seems adequate to assess a period hallmarked by a major international financial crisis.

Case selection

CEE tends to have relatively short-lived cabinets compared to Western Europe (Keman and Müller-Rommel 2012; Savage 2013). Nevertheless, as Hungary mostly had "cabinets fulfilling their complete term ", "government stability has not been a problem" for a country, which is often-times explicitly described in the literature as "an exception to the rule" (Grotz and Weber 2012, 699; Bergman, Ersson, and Hellström 2015, 368). The constructive vote of no-confidence (CVNC) acted as a powerful institutional factor to keep PMs and their party governments in office (Nikolenyi 2004, 133), whereas the highly polarised two-bloc system characterising pre-2010 Hungarian politics (Kovarek and Soós 2016) encouraged parties to "interact within a narrow ideological range" and restricted their coalition choices (Savage 2013, 1032).

Consequently, Hungary stands as the only CEE country where the cabinets' survival rate is more than half of the legislative period (Keman and Müller-Rommel 2012, 15), as shown in Table 1. The fact that governments in Hungary serve out most of their term is notwithstanding a by-product of the preponderance of majority governments, associated with higher levels of stability (Somer-Topcu and Williams 2008; Grotz and Weber 2012; Bergman, Ersson, and Hellström 2015). Unlike the rest of CEE, minority cabinets in Hungary have been much less common phenomena; nevertheless, they could rely on the CVNC (for survival) and extensive negative agenda control powers (for passing or blocking legislations). Governing majorities can control not only the floor, but can block proposals already at the committee stage (Zubek 2011), characteristics known for enhancing minority cabinet success (Field 2009, 423).

Table 1. PMs and party governments in Hungary (1990–2019).

Cabinet	Date in	Date out	PM duration	Cabinet duration	Party composition	Cabinet type
Antall	1990-05-23	1993-12-12	1320	1320	**MDF**-FKGP-KDNP	SUR
Boross	1993-12-21	1994-05-29	160	160	**MDF**-FKGP-KDNP	SUR
Horn	1994-07-15	1998-05-24	1410	1410	**MSZP**-SZDSZ	SUR
Orbán I	1998-07-06	2002-04-21	1386	1386	**Fidesz**-FKGP-MDF	MWC
Medgyessy	2002-05-27	2004-08-25	822	822	**MSZP**-SZDSZ	MWC
Gyurcsány I	2004-10-04	2006-04-23	1607	567	**MSZP**-SZDSZ	MWC
Gyurcsány II	2006-06-09	2008-04-30		692	**MSZP**-SZDSZ	MWC
Gyurcsány III	2008-05-02	2009-04-14		348	**MSZP**	MIN
Bajnai	2009-04-14	2010-04-25	377	377	**MSZP**	MIN
Orbán II	2010-05-29	2014-04-06	3432	1409	**Fidesz**-KDNP	SUR
Orbán III	2014-05-10	2018-04-08		1430	**Fidesz**-KDNP	SUR
Orbán IV	2018-05-18			593	**Fidesz**-KDNP	SUR

Source: Author's compilation. MIN: minority; MWC: minimal winning coalition; SUR: surplus coalition. PM and cabinet duration for Orbán IV are calculated until 2019-12-31.

Besides institutional factors, contextual ones like the PMs' significant role in determining their cabinets' policy agenda also enabled effective policy performance of minority governments. This allows to scrutinise strategies PMs might pursue in order to secure legislative backing. Curini and Hino (2012) suggest that whenever parties expect minority cabinets to be formed, they position themselves near the centre with the aim to accommodate demands of parties, which are likely to provide external support in the legislative arena. Given the exceptional powers of Hungarian PMs and their unequivocal role in determining cabinets' policy agenda, it is not an unreasonable assumption that the same calculus (rather) applies to PMs themselves. When economic crises incentivise politicians to forge *ad hoc* coalitions with MPs of otherwise juxtaposed parties (Pastorella 2016), who would be better suited to signal shifting policy or ideological positions than PMs declaring crisis management as their highest priority?

In this paper, I compare Hungary's only two minority cabinets: the one led by Ferenc Gyurcsány (2008–2009) and the one headed by his direct successor, Gordon Bajnai (2009–2010). The institutional and political context was essentially identical for both cabinets and their tenure lasted for approximately the same time.[1] Both cabinets undertook to solve a deep economic crisis and were "under permanent pressure from the opposition ", as Fidesz-KDNP[2] and MDF questioned these governments' legitimacy, urged the dissolution of the National Assembly, called for snap elections and aimed to block the budget (Stumpf 2009, 475; Körösényi, Ondré, and Hajdú 2017, 97). They were single-party minority governments, backed by MPs of the Hungarian Socialist Party (MSZP). MSZP had 190 MPs in the National Assembly, but needed 194 votes for an absolute majority. Theoretically, this could have been secured with the five independent MPs, eliminating the need to bargain with opposition parties. However, the diverse ideological background of independents made it an unlikely scenario. Furthermore, two Socialist MPs were permanently hospitalised with severe illness, effectively reducing the minority government's plurality to 188.

Consequently, MSZP primarily relied on the external support of the SZDSZ, which declared its intention to become a "constructive opposition" party, and support only bills which are in accordance with its liberal values. These parties have governed together between 2002 and 2008 and have also been in power between 1994 and 1998. Party concentration, the effective number of parliamentary parties, ideological cohesiveness of cabinets (Bergman, Ersson, and Hellström 2015, 364) or party system polarisation are also held constant under Gyurcsány and Bajnai.

In the Hungarian case, *positional agenda power* cannot explain differences in cabinet performance. Both cabinets of Gyurcsány and Bajnai were built on MSZP, but the Socialists were nowhere near being a party with a central position. Quite contrarily, they occupied the left extreme of the party system, an unfavourable spatial position for minority cabinets, as it hinders governments' ability to pass legislation with shifting alliances, negotiated on an *ad hoc* basis. If location in the centre of the ideological space is a prerequisite for minority cabinets to govern effectively, neither case of this study had a shot to perform well.

Ideological proximity, on the other hand, is more likely to be associated with different levels of minority cabinets' policy performance. Whereas MSZP could not trade off the leftmost position in the party system for a median one from 2008 to 2009, it was potentially more feasible to diminish the distance between Socialists and SZDSZ, MDF or Fidesz. The question is, how to capture government-opposition divisiveness (Klüver and Zubek 2018) for each minority cabinet?

I hypothesise that difference in *policy performance* stems from dissimilar *partisan background of PMs*. MSZP had no bipolar opposition to rely on when securing legislative backing; consequently, the party was doomed to gravitate towards the centre with respect to its ideological stance on economic and social issues alike. In the absence of snap elections, manifestos and pledges, incumbent PMs remained the only political actors who could authentically represent MSZP's spatial position. According to this assumption, the closer these heads of governments were to the center, the more likely opposition (SZDSZ, MDF or Fidesz) MPs were to support government-initiated bills and motions.

Centrist heuristics potentially made it more appealing for MPs to lend external support to Gyurcsány or Bajnai, who were otherwise hesitant to endorse left-wing causes and had no interest in restoring MSZP's competent image. In exchange for sustaining minority cabinets, SZDSZ or MDF could strategically count on benefitting from particular, long-desired policies, while not sharing the blame associated with unpopular policies (Sitter 2011). This way, they could have avoided being scapegoated for austerity measures deemed necessary for crisis management. It took ideologically aligned policies – that is, ones more right-wing than MSZP's economic (or cultural) position – to support (some of) the government's agenda. If this argument is corroborated by empirical evidence, we see *a higher number of opposition MPs* lending external support to the PM *closer to the centre*, subsequently enabling his cabinet to *perform better*.

The rest of the alternative explanations, discussed in the previous section, are either implausible in the Hungarian context or describe an institutional feature held constant. Multilevel dynamics bear little relevance, as Hungary is a centralised, unitary state with a weak regional level, where regional actors have no veto power (or even representation) in the unicameral parliament. As full-scale cooperation of opposition parties has remained an unrealistic scenario throughout both cabinets' tenure, alternative majorities had no room to develop. Bloc politics have undoubtedly hallmarked Hungary, and voters were quick to punish parties abandoning (or failing to position themselves in relation to) either of the two blocs.[3] But as the National Assembly's partisan composition is unchanged in the MSSD framework, this cannot yield differences in cabinet performance. The ideological polarisation of party platforms reached extreme levels in Hungary (Vegetti 2019, 79), but while we lack empirical data to contrast consecutive cabinets, it would also be unrealistic to expect seismic changes over the course of just a year. If polarisation undermined policy performance, it did so for both governments.

One could posit that the poor policy performance of Gyurcsány's minority cabinet is primarily linked to his history of conflict with the liberals. Whereas a myriad of conflicts indeed existed between the Socialist PM and SZDSZ politicians, Bajnai had a far more troublesome relationship with Socialist MPs. Many feared that Bajnai's inexorable attitude on spotlessness and legality of EU grants (Lakner et al. 2019, 23) impedes speedy delivery of infrastructural developments, undermining their chances of re-election in their single-member districts (SMDs). As such MSZP politicians have outnumbered the *entire* SZDSZ parliamentary group, the "legacy of unresolved conflicts and personal frictions" (Chiru 2015, 170) should have posed a larger challenge to Bajnai than to his predecessor. Lastly, at least some SZDSZ MPs must have cultivated a close, loyal relationship with

Gyurcsány – as demonstrated by the fact that a handful of them joined his splinter party after 2011, following the electoral annihilation and dissolution of SZDSZ.

Political career of Gyurcsány and Bajnai

Similitudes aside, there is one key difference between the two governments: their leaders' partisan embeddedness and background. Gyurcsány's political career is often described as "meteoric," as – relying on his charisma and extraordinary political skills – he rose from backbencher to PM in just four years (Körösényi, Ondré, and Hajdú 2017). Although he always had strong family links to the MSZP, he formally entered politics only in 2001 (a year after he joined the party), as a member of Péter Medgyessy's campaign team. Once appointed as Minister of Sports and Youth Affairs, he used his cabinet position to harness support at the grassroots and subsequently obtained the chairmanship of a county-level party unit, one of the key positions in MSZP's decentralised organisational structure (Kovarek and Soós 2016). After Medgyessy's resignation, Gyurcsány defeated a long-time MSZP strongman in an intra-party fight and succeeded Medgyessy as PM in 2004 (Körösényi, Ondré, and Hajdú 2017). Breaking the cycles of "hyper-accountability" (Roberts 2008), Gyurcsány has become the first incumbent PM who could secure re-election in 2006.

Gyurcsány's political career suffered a serious blow in Fall 2006, when – just months after introducing austerity measures – a speech he made in front of MSZP central party figures was leaked out, in which he admitted lying to the public and covering up the state of the economy. Large-scale protests and riots, as well as subsequent police brutality sinked his approval ratings and eroded most of his leadership capital. Losing a referendum initiated by the opposition against the coalition's reforms in March 2008 paved the way for intra-cabinet tensions and SZDSZ's departure (Körösényi, Ondré, and Hajdú 2017), leaving MSZP to govern alone, as the first minority cabinet in post-communist Hungary. His resignation came only a year later, when the first waves of the sovereign debt crisis hit Hungary and Gyurcsány felt that his crisis-management plan lacks both intra-party and popular support.

Bajnai, quite contrarily, spent almost all of his career in business, acting as managing director and CEO of various investment companies. He was invited to Gyurcsány's cabinet in 2007 to administer allocation of EU funds as Minister of Local Government and Regional Development. In this role, he often came into conflict with MSZP mayors and regional strongmen, as Bajnai was known for his staunch opposition to incomplete, inaccurate and potentially rigged or corrupt grant applications (Lakner et al. 2019).

He assumed his office as PM on 16 April 2009 following a CVNC, nearly a month after Gyurcsány has announced his resignation. To convince international markets, he shortly introduced a robust austerity package worth 1000 Billion HUF, including measures of tax raises, curbing social benefits, raising retirement age and cutting pensions, as well as wage freezes for public employees (Illés and Körösényi 2017). Before assuming office, he forced Socialist and liberal MPs to sign a political declaration, committing themselves to support his legislative agenda (Lakner et al. 2019, 184). This "contract" had likely made his future cabinet more credible for financial markets and also restored some of the public's confidence in the Socialist party.

Measuring prime ministers' ideological position

It is challenging to locate Bajnai and Gyurcsány in the ideological space. Whereas measurements are usually available for party manifestos published before elections, neither minority cabinet was preceded by a snap election. PMs usually compete as parliamentary candidates, but responses on self-declared ideological positions of incumbents and challengers are routinely anonymised before publishing.

Measuring cabinets' position is a similarly hard nut to crack. At almost all times, expert surveys only ask parties' ideological position; even when datasets report cabinets' location on unidimensional scales, scores are usually computed as a weighted mean or median position of cabinet parties (Döring and Schwander 2015). Expert surveys are abundant on measuring PMs' performance, but there's none capturing cabinet heads' position on dimensions like RILE or GALTAN (Volkens et al. 2019). This leaves us with no other choice, but to compare Gyurcsány's and Bajnai's left-right (or liberal-conservative) position qualitatively, with an extensive review of the international and Hungarian literature on these two PMs' ideological character.

Described as the "champion" and "hero" of the left-liberal electorate, Gyurcsány undertook to renew MSZP and left-wing politics in Hungary, a vision inspired by Tony Blair's Third Way approach. Appearing as a moderniser, who is "trying to create a new synthesis of Hungarian liberalism and the new social democracy ", he was also elected as chairman of the Socialist Party, a position to which he was re-elected even after his resignation as PM (Körösényi, Ondré, and Hajdú 2017, 89–90). Gyurcsány put forward a "strong political vision" and was determined to revamp MSZP's intellectual hinterland, authoring books and founding a progressive think tank.

Contextual factors have also pulled Gyurcsány away from the centre, making his (cabinet's) character a markedly leftist one. These include ideological pressure from central party figures of MSZP and the desire to distinguish Socialists from liberals after the coalition break-up. Gyurcsány had to maintain a delicate balance vis-á-vis MSZP strongmen. In January 2009, an influential MP published an op-ed, advocating for the left-wing turn of the party, criticising "neoliberal politics" and demanding taxation of "bankers and brokers ". The op-ed was surprisingly well-received by MSZP ministers and board members, but its pamphlet-style made it hard to operationalise its demands as policies (Ripp 2010, 39).

The genesis of Gyurcsány's minority cabinet is also understood as his decision to sacrifice the coalition for maintaining Socialist MPs and central party figures' support via rejecting liberal reforms. For this, he had to revive MSZP's traditional image and protect social interests. After losing the referendum, Gyurcsány turned the liberal Minister of Health a scapegoat, depicting his own cabinet's unpopular reforms as if they have been imposed upon the Socialists (and voters) by the SZDSZ. This allowed Gyurcsány to secure his political hinterland (MSZP politicians cheerfully welcomed the "long-awaited liberation" as the coalition was terminated) and also offered an opportunity to liberals for repositioning themselves as ardent defenders of market-friendly reforms. Socialist

PRIME MINISTERS AND PARTY GOVERNMENTS IN CENTRAL AND EASTERN EUROPE   59

politicians were hoping to strengthen MSZP's left-wing character after the break-up, allowing to win back some of their former voters.

Gyurcsány's tax cut plan, for instance, exemplifies the diverging policy position of former coalition partners. Whereas it was an attempt to secure liberals' support for the budget, the plan remained unacceptable for SZDSZ. Worth less than 0.5% of GDP and financed from tax raises on other domains, the proposal was expected to have no meaningful stimulus effect (Stumpf 2009, 484–485).

Unlike Gyurcsány, Bajnai had a "somewhat apolitical character" (Illés 2014, 11): he never joined MSZP and had no family ties to the party either. He reluctantly labelled himself as a "liberal-social democrat" and "social-liberal" (Lakner et al. 2019, 180), but reiterated on multiple occasions that "the crisis does not have a worldview" and the Hungarian currency has "no party preference" either (Illés 2014, 12).

Bajnai and Gyurcsány had also articulated markedly different positions in a handful of symbolic issues. One example is the issue of diaspora Hungarians. Whereas Bajnai was receptive to Fidesz's proposal of granting Hungarian citizenship (without voting rights) to ethnic Hungarians living in neighbouring countries, a long-cherished idea of right-wing publics in Hungary, socialist-liberal politicians and intellectuals had an ambivalent relationship with diaspora Hungarians. While in office, Gyurcsány has campaigned *against* extending citizenship rights at the referendum of 2004; his splinter party Democratic Coalition (DK) remains the only relevant party in contemporary Hungary vigorously opposing voting rights of diaspora Hungarians, even pledging to disenfranchise them. Contrarily, Bajnai has attempted (unsuccessfully) to convince MSZP leaders to support the Fidesz-initiated bill in Parliament in 2009.

Contrasting the PMs' visits in the Vatican is a good proxy for their position on church-state relations. Meeting Pope John Paul II in 2004, Gyurcsány used the opportunity to scold the Hungarian Catholic Church for interfering in domestic politics and incentivising schoolchildren to protest against the government. This triggered the outrage of Fidesz politicians, accusing Gyurcsány of juxtaposing believers and non-believers. Conversely, disagreements and critiques were absent from Bajnai's visit to Pope Benedict XVI. Bilateral relations were described as "strong and balanced"; Bajnai thanked the Church for "solidarity and support" shown during the economic crisis and even raised the issue of Catholic diaspora Hungarians (Népszabadság 2009).

Furthermore, Bajnai has abandoned MSZP's traditional position when he attempted to speed up publishing the names of those having worked for the domestic secret police as informers during communist years. His platform resembled that of SZDSZ, which used to be the most ardent supporter of agent file transparency. This has only become more prominent after the Fidesz-initiated anti-government populist referendum in 2008. SZDSZ was campaigning on anti-Socialist platform (twisting Fidesz's "social referendum ", using the slogan "Say no to Socialism!"), aiming to win over not just *economically* right-wing voters, but also anti-communist ones. Responding to pressure from liberals, Gyurcsány also aimed to appear as a proponent of disclosing these information, but his position remained inconsistent. His cabinet narrowed down the scope of names to be published, and Socialists have voted down bills on lustration and transparency of post-1956 documents under Gyurcsány's tenure, questioning his genuine commitment on the matter.

These examples illustrate how Bajnai endorsed issues and policies traditionally characterised by right-wing parties' issue ownership. This is not to say that Gyurcsány did not attempt to forge (legislative) alliances across the two camps, spanning traditional cleavages: his op-ed titled "Agreement" (*Megegyezés*) is understood as an effort "not only to win SZDSZ over, but also to pacify Fidesz" via integrating some of the latter's favoured policies into the PM's manifesto (Csizmadia 2009, 510–511).

As both cabinets were self-declared "reform" and "crisis management" governments, I shall review the PMs' economic position before moving on to evaluate the policy performance of their cabinets. Gyurcsány's minority government has "turned back to the traditional policy line of the MSZP" (Körösényi, Ondré, and Hajdú 2017, 94). Abandoning tax cuts and privatisation – policies he once favoured –, Gyurcsány "stood to the left of *all* parliamentary parties in economic questions" (Tóth and Török 2015, 286). As Tóth and Török put it, shifting economic (and social) positions was a major tool for him to consolidate power. Leaving his market-friendly, liberal-progressive image behind, Gyurcsány attempted to recover the left-wing electorate's trust by deliberately pulling away from the economic-ideological center. Contrarily, Bajnai embraced solutions suggested by the dominant neoliberal economic paradigm and actors like IMF or the European Central Bank, primarily aiming to restore credibility vis-á-vis Hungary's creditors (Illés and Körösényi 2017).

Bajnai's centrist strategy also included defining himself as a technocrat, a label also oftentimes used in the literature. Sitter (2011) considers his cabinet as "a more or less technocratic interim government" and Pastorella (2016) also lists Bajnai's cabinet among technocratic governments.

However, it does *not* qualify as a "full technocratic government" according to the definition of McDonnell and Valbruzzi (2014) ("cabinet composed of all non-partisan, expert ministers and headed by a non-partisan prime minister"), as it was "dominantly built on the old ministers [of Gyurcsány] and projected the image of a traditional political government" (Stumpf 2010, 139). Bajnai did not only keep some of Gyurcsány's Socialist ministers (hoping that it could facilitate cooperation with the party's parliamentary group and make MSZP "personally" interested in his success), but also appointed MSZP members to portfolios previously held by non-partisan politicians (e.g. Minister of Local Government).

Furthermore, cabinet compositions are to be interpreted in the context they operate. Hungarian governments consistently had a high proportion of experts: 41% of all ministerial appointments brought an expert into cabinet (Ilonszki and Stefan 2018). The conduciveness of Hungarian politics for participation of experts in government partly stems from PMs' discretionary powers to appoint (and dismiss) ministers and intention to strengthen their position vis-á-vis their own parties and coalition partners. It also reflects a longer tradition, rooted in Hungary's pre-transition regime, which did not only tolerate, but oftentimes demanded expertise at the highest levels, appointing so-called "reform economists" to key positions of its late governments (Ilonszki and Stefan 2018, 206).

Moreover, Bajnai lacked a "sufficiently broad mandate" (Pastorella 2016, 949) for implementing his program. 204 MPs promised to pass his legislative agenda in writing, but the definition implies a broader coalition behind technocratic leaders – "widespread, cross-partisan support" for a "government of national unity ", as Pastorella (2016, 953) would put it –, and opposition actors' commitment not to reverse policies. Bajnai could claim none of the above.

I argue that Bajnai has led a *"simulated technocratic government"*, where he acted as if *all* of his cabinet members were experts and in a manner as if he would have broad, cross-partisan legislative backing that transcends traditional cleavages. Bajnai insisted on not having "a political ambition", and sought to appoint experts to the key positions of his government, who similarly have solely professional drives (Illés 2014, 12). Moreover, SZDSZ has been advocating for an "expert government" since fall 2008. These efforts to create the illusion of a technocratic government made it harder for the liberals to reject the investiture of Bajnai's cabinet.

Nevertheless, as neither having a non-partisan politician to lead an MSZP government, nor the strong presence of expert ministers in cabinets was unusual in Hungary (Ilonszki and Stefan 2018), government and opposition actors have equally treated Bajnai as a traditional, partisan PM. He emphasised the need for "consent and national concordance" (Illés 2014, 13) and beliefs that "Hungary's interest would be best served by a grand coalition, or a social contract of similar value" (Lakner et al. 2019, 181), but these statements only expressed his desires, but not parliamentary arithmetics and political realities. His self-perceived position has important implications for securing legislative backing for his program, but shall not prevent me from comparing his cabinet with Gyurcsány's last one in a MSSD framework.

One could argue that Bajnai distanced himself from MSZP only to save the party from negative externalities of crisis-management policies, such as diminishing favourability ratings. On the contrary, he always believed that maintaining an image of competent and potent governance could have helped the Socialists' campaign in 2010 – if they were to associate themselves (more) with his tenure and fiscal achievements (Lakner et al. 2019). The PM also avoided attacking all parties but one: far-right Jobbik, the only relevant extra-parliamentary party from which he could expect no external support. Similarly vigorous negative campaigns of other opposition parties (e.g. Fidesz tried to directly associate him with suicides of farmers, which happened during Bajnai's tenure as CEO) were left without retorts from Bajnai's side.

Measuring cabinet performance

Given their formation context, neither of the two cabinets had a formal government program or manifesto, making it impossible to assess their performance with indicators like legislative reliability.

Therefore, I start by conducting a quantitative analysis of the legislative success of governments. Using original data obtained from the official website of the National Assembly (parlament.hu) via webscraping, I first matched a dataset on proposals ($N = 16,264$) with another on voting record of MPs ($N = 2,466,175$), collected for period between 1 May 2008 and 29 May 2010. I then restricted the scope to *bills initiated by the government* or *a minister*, excluding proposals such as private member's bills or amendments to the Standing Orders. Subsequently, I calculated the *percentage of government bills presented that are approved*, as well as the *partisan composition of external support* to scrutinise legislator voting behaviour and alliance shifting.

Table 2 demonstrates that Bajnai's cabinet indeed performed better in the absolute and relative number of government-initiated bills. Even after restricting the scope to bills passed with *less than 300 votes* – a rule-of-thumb threshold for merely symbolic or technical proposals – Gyurcsány is outperformed by his successor. Bajnai consistently faring better among Socialist MPs is striking – and hints that despite his queen sacrifice, Gyurcsány will be unable to keep party control. On average, the non-partisan PM also obtained the support of more liberal MPs, whereas his cabinet was more rejected by MDF's conservative legislators.

These results suggest at least two potential mechanisms. First, the written agreement Bajnai enforced on MPs was possibly perceived as (morally) binding by some MPs who were otherwise reluctant to support Gyurcsány's agenda. Furthermore, his economically liberal policies were relatively well-received by SZDSZ parliamentarians. Results are more mixed for MDF and independents. Descriptions of Gyurcsány securing majority via "buying" independent legislators with favours (Stumpf 2009, 489) and Bajnai sacking the sole independent MP, who obtained a SMD mandate and served as Minister of Local Government under his predecessor could potentially explain some of the variation in the latter.

To expand the analysis, I continue with presenting qualitative assessments of these cabinets, collected via a systematic review of Hungarian and international literature. Scholars more or less agree that Gyurcsány's minority cabinet performed poorly, as reforms concerning several policy areas have failed or were overturned; even some measures of Gyurcsány's previous (i.e. majority) government were withdrawn (Körösényi, Ondré, and Hajdú 2017). Gyurcsány's minority cabinet received the lowest average performance value from respondents of a recent expert survey, conducted among Hungarian political scientists and historians (Grotz et al. 2019). Budget deficit and sovereign debt have heavily increased during Gyurcsány's tenure; as Sitter (2011, 4) eloquently put it, "consistent and prudent economic policy took a lower priority than re-election ". By remaining overly focused on consolidating his intra-party position, Gyurcsány "could not manage the economic crisis; not because he lacked competence or vision on how to solve it, but because neither markets, nor voters believed in his proposals," as he had "insufficient political power to push them through" (Tóth and Török 2015, 298). Despite SZDSZ and MDF both endorsing policy proposals of the *Reform Alliance*,[4] Gyurcsány rather (unsuccessfully) sought support for his own austerity measures (Ripp 2010) and the cabinet was constantly running behind its schedule (Stumpf 2009, 477).

Whereas Gyurcsány's efforts to demonstrate competence and manage the crisis ended in failure, the verdict on his successor's performance tends to be more favourable, whether made by political scientists or the wide public (Csizmadia 2009). Comparing the two governments, Simonovits (2016, 294) describes Gyurcsány's cabinet as one

Table 2. Government-initiated bills passed in the National Assembly under minority cabinets.

	Gyurcsány (2008–2009)	Bajnai (2009–2010)
Passed (N)	534	1237
Passed (%)	89	95
Passed (<300 votes, N)	340	1043
Passed (<300 votes, %)	84	94
MSZP votes (μ)	171.4	175.0
SZDSZ votes (μ)	11.2	12.2
MDF votes (μ)	5.3	2.6
Independent votes (μ)	1.7	1.4

Source: Author's own calculations.

lacking "sufficient determination to cut expenditures ", being reluctant to implement necessary pension reforms "even at the peak of the crisis ". Contrarily, he approves Bajnai's measures on retirement age, price indexation, employers' pension contribution rate and the 13th month benefit, and deems freezing and cutting wages in the public sector adequate and "spectacular ". Bajnai "has improved the quality of governance" (Tóth and Török 2015, 373) and regained the confidence of markets and brought stability. As Illés and Körösényi (2017) put it, his policies were successful from the fiscal point of view, nonetheless they did not improve re-election chances of parties supporting his government.

Passing the budget is often viewed as one of the greatest challenges minority cabinets face, as well as a key indicator of their success. Gyurcsány could whip all Socialist MPs to support the proposal and he also harnessed the support of one MDF and two "independent" MPs – serving as minister and prime-ministerial commissioner, respectively –, but the bill would not have passed without the absence of two other MPs. Bajnai commanded a larger majority, with all Socialist MPs but one, as well as 13 SZDSZ and one independent legislators supporting the budget. Sárközy (2012, 365) commends the budget proposed by Bajnai (and the "relative ease" of its passing in Parliament), whereas others highlight how successful his cabinet was in uncovering municipal or government corruption and financial misuse (Csaba 2012, 11). The cabinet also introduced two major legal changes: it passed a new Civil Code and enacted a law on registered partnerships, essentially providing nearly all the benefits of marriage to same-sex couples. Bajnai's centrist orientation also helped him to restore a relationship of mutual trust with the President of the Republic (Sárközy 2012, 366), a nexus characterised by deep animosity under his predecessor's tenure.

Cabinets' foreign policy performance also varies. Hungarian–Slovak relations were at historic lows under their tenure: Slovakia passed a bill to prohibit public use of Hungarian language and banned the President of Hungary from entering its territory. Both Gyurcsány and Bajnai held meetings with PM Robert Fico, yielding outcomes of differing success (Népszabadság 2008; Šutaj 2014).

Gyurcsány put forward a proposal of combatting extremism and (mutual) protection of minority rights, all six points of which were publicly rejected and ridiculed by Fico. Almost exactly a year later, another meeting was concluded by Fico agreeing with all 11 points drafted by the Bajnai cabinet, including largely similar (and mostly symbolic) declarations. The Slovak PM also agreed to follow the recommendations of OSCE with respect to amending the language law and expressed regret over banning President Sólyom. Pundits have interpreted the latter meeting as "leaving rock bottom behind ". For achieving this, Bajnai heavily relied on his expert Minister of Foreign Affairs, a distinguished professor of IR, who held high-level political positions under both left and right-wing governments.

Bajnai's cabinet could pass more bills, both in relative and absolute terms. Nevertheless, the difference is smaller than what poor evaluations of Gyurcsány's minority cabinet would imply. Results suggest that legislative performance is not (necessarily) the most important indicator of (minority) cabinets' performance according to the judgement of scholars and the wide public. Equivalence of different performance measures (policymaking, legislative success, approval ratings, governing party's record in the next election) warrants direct examination by future research.

Conclusion

The article investigated the policy performance of Hungary's two minority cabinets by utilising a MSSD framework. A qualitative review of Gyurcsány's and Bajnai's economic and ideological position was followed by an analysis of MPs' voting record in the National Assembly. The empirical results have provided support for the relationship between the PMs' ideological position and their ability to secure legislative majorities. Consequently, the paper may be viewed as offering some empirical evidence for the *ideological proximity* hypothesis (Klüver and Zubek 2018): MSZP could not abandon its extreme position within the party system, but Bajnai consciously positioned himself closer to SZDSZ and MDF parliamentarians.

These findings expand our knowledge on performance of cabinets and PMs in CEE. Hungary's minority governments have hitherto not been subject to empirical scrutiny, despite administering serious policy changes and tackling one of the worst economic setbacks the country has seen for decades. These cases broaden our understanding of party governments without legislative majorities in CEE. Minority cabinets occur relatively frequently in the region (Zubek 2011), but remain understudied in comparative politics. The investigated cabinets share more with other Hungarian cases than with extensively researched minority governments in Denmark, Sweden or Spain. Whereas latter cases are tales of securing legislative backing from both sides of the aisle, external support in polarised party systems of CEE is often restricted to a single flank of the parliament.

In a similar fashion, the literature on minority cabinets in countries with positive parliamentarism, a macro-institutional environment fostering government stability and effectiveness and strongly majoritarian electoral systems is almost entirely absent. Findings address this gap: to improve our understanding of the structural and contextual reasons behind Hungary having had almost exclusively multi-party, majority governments, the study provided an in-depth analysis of deviant cases, i.e. the only two instances of single-party, minority cabinets.

Corroborating findings on Spain (Field 2009), the analysis helps us to better understand survival and performance of minority governments in majoritarian contexts. It seems that governments' tight control of the parliamentary agenda, the CVNC or PMs' discretionary powers do not impede the creation of minority cabinets, but rather *sustain* them once they are formed.

This article also extends previous work on how pre-electoral agreements affect cabinet survival and performance. Bajnai, still as a Prime Minister-elect, made MPs to declare their support for core parts of his legislative agenda in writing. Further research needs to examine the effects of such agreements and the contexts in which they are formed, whether they be forged between future coalition partners (Chiru 2015), government parties and independent MPs (Kefford and Weeks 2018) or between pre-investiture executives and members of the legislatures.

At a theoretical level, the paper furthermore contributes by clarifying the character of Bajnai's cabinet. Whereas a large part of the literature had difficulties to classify it,[5] most scholars labelled it as a "technocratic" government. Demonstrating how Bajnai lacked wide, cross-partisan support and how his cabinet's room for manoeuver was restricted by entrenched, bipolar competition, I showed the "simulated" nature of its technocratic character. It was a conscious attempt to pull towards the center and make (policies of) his cabinet more likely to be supported by SZDSZ and MDF parliamentarians.

PRIME MINISTERS AND PARTY GOVERNMENTS IN CENTRAL AND EASTERN EUROPE 65

I argued that differences in performance can be associated with distinct strategies of PMs to ideologically position themselves. In relation to the literature on the " presidentialisation" of politics in CEE (Hloušek 2015; Berz 2019), the findings above also stress PMs' elevated role – in electoral, party and parliamentary arenas alike. Further research would benefit from systematic data collection on ideological position of governments and PMs, and should evaluate the degree to which median or ideologically proximate position of PMs – relative to other parties – shape legislative behaviour and influence government performance in other CEE countries.

Notes

1. Gyurcsány originally having twice the remaining office time would cause problems for cabinet *survival* analysis, but should not influence policy performance. It can be contended that Gyurcsány was hesitant to introduce comprehensive reforms (and passed fewer bills), because he deliberately postponed austerity measures to the end of his term. However, this seems unlikely: pushing them closer to April 2010 and idly witnessing the economic crisis to expand would have been electoral suicide for the PM, who – unlike Bajnai – was seeking reelection.
2. KDNP stands for *Christian Democratic People's Party*; as a small satellite party of Fidesz, it allows and encourages dual membership, its MPs sit in a joint Fidesz-KDNP parliamentary group, strictly following party discipline. It has not contested any election alone since 1998 (Kovarek and Soós 2016).
3. In 2010, MDF has failed to pass the 5% parliamentary threshold after it selected a former Socialist minister as lead candidate and forged an electoral alliance with the liberals. LMP lost most of its voters and became irrelevant in 2018, following a half-year long turmoil emerging as a consequence of the party's isolationist wing taking revenge on MPs and co-chairs advocating for closer electoral co-operation with left-liberal parties (Kovarek and Littvay 2019).
4. A group of economists, industrialists and academics, whose manifesto was later largely incorporated into Bajnai's legislative agenda.
5. As Ilonszki and Stefan (2018, 212) aptly wrote, whereas "half of Bajnai's ministers" were experts, his cabinet's "fundamental party support makes it a borderline case".

Acknowledgments

The author would like to thank Bálint Kubik who has provided invaluable technical support for data collection. He is grateful to Florian Grotz, Jan Berz, Mažvydas Jastramskis, Marko Kukec, Zsolt Enyedi and Maria Spirova for their helpful comments on an earlier version of this paper. Healthy skepticism and sharp insights of Peter Visnovitz have substantially improved the study.

Disclosure statement

No potential conflict of interest was reported by the author(s).

ORCID

Daniel Kovarek ⓘ http://orcid.org/0000-0002-3385-3742

References

Alexiadou, Despina. 2015. "Ideologues, Partisans, and Loyalists: Cabinet Ministers and Social Welfare Reform in Parliamentary Democracies." *Comparative Political Studies* 48 (8): 1051–1086.

Bergman, Torbjörn, Svante Ersson, and Johan Hellström. 2015. "Government Formation and Breakdown in Western and Central Eastern Europe." *Comparative European Politics* 13 (3): 345–375.

Berz, Jan. 2019. "Potent Executives: The Electoral Strength of Prime Ministers in Central Eastern Europe." *East European Politics* 35 (4): 517–537.

Chiru, Mihail. 2015. "Early Marriages Last Longer: Pre-electoral Coalitions and Government Survival in Europe." *Government and Opposition* 50 (2): 165–188.

Cody, Howard. 2008. "Minority Government in Canada: The Stephen Harper Experience." *American Review of Canadian Studies* 38 (1): 27–42.

Csaba, László. 2012. "Haladás vagy elmaradás? Avagy miért marad le Magyarország." In *Földobott kő? Tények és tendenciák a 21. században*, edited by László Muraközy, 282–312. Budapest: Akadémiai Kiadó.

Csizmadia, Ervin. 2009. "A konszenzus gondolata a 2008. évi kormánypolitikában." In *Magyarország politikai évkönyve 2008-ról*, edited by Péter Sándor and László Vass. Budapest: DKMKA.

Curini, Luigi, and Airo Hino. 2012. "Missing Links in Party-System Polarization: How Institutions and Voters Matter." *The Journal of Politics* 74 (2): 460–473.

Döring, Holger, and Hanna Schwander. 2015. "Revisiting the Left Cabinet Share: How to Measure the Partisan Profile of Governments in Welfare State Research." *Journal of European Social Policy* 25 (2): 175–193.

Field, Bonnie N. 2009. "Minority Government and Legislative Politics in a Multilevel State: Spain Under Zapatero." *South European Society and Politics* 14 (4): 417–434.

Green-Pedersen, Christoffer. 2001. "Minority Governments and Party Politics: The Political and Institutional Background to the 'Danish Miracle'." *Journal of Public Policy* 21 (1): 53–70.

Green-Pedersen, Christoffer, and Lisbeth Hoffmann Thomsen. 2005. "Bloc Politics Vs. Broad Cooperation? The Functioning of Danish Minority Parliamentarism." *The Journal of Legislative Studies* 11 (2): 153–169.

Grotz, Florian, Ferdinand Müller-Rommel, Jan Berz, Corinna Kröber, and Marko Kukec. 2019. "Explaining Prime-Ministerial Performance: Evidence from Central and Eastern Europe." Paper presented at General Conference of ECPR, Wrocław, Poland.

Grotz, Florian, and Till Weber. 2012. "Party Systems and Government Stability in Central and Eastern Europe." *World Politics* 64 (4): 699–740.

Helms, Ludger 2020. "Performance and Evaluation of Political Executives." In *The Oxford Handbook of Political Executives*, edited by Rudy B. Andeweg, Robert Elgie, Ludger Helms, Juliet Kaarbo, and Ferdinand Müller-Rommel, 646–670. Oxford: Oxford University Press.

Hloušek, Vít. 2015. "Two Types of Presidentialization in the Party Politics of Central Eastern Europe." *Italian Political Science Review/Rivista Italiana di Scienza Politica* 45 (3): 277–299.

Illés, Gábor. 2014. "Interpretive Leadership. The Use of Political Discourse in Crises." Paper presented at ECPR Graduate Student Conference, University of Innsbruck. http://ecpr.eu/Events/PaperDetails.aspx?PaperID=16816&EventID=13

Illés, Gábor, and András Körösényi. 2017. "Ortodoxia, heterodoxia és cselekvés: Bajnai Gordon és Orbán Viktor válságkezelése, 2009–2014." In *Viharban kormányozni. Politikai vezetök válsághelyzetekben*, edited by András Körösényi, 139–166. Budapest: MTA TK PTI.

Ilonszki, Gabriella, and Laurentiu Stefan. 2018. "Variations in the Expert Ministerial Framework in Hungary and Romania: Personal and Institutional Explanations." In *Technocratic Ministers and Political Leadership in European Democracies*, edited by António Costa Pinto, Maurizio Cotta, and Pedro Tavares de Almeida, 203–233. Cham: Palgrave Macmillan.

PRIME MINISTERS AND PARTY GOVERNMENTS IN CENTRAL AND EASTERN EUROPE

Kefford, Glenn, and Liam Weeks. 2018. "Minority Party Government and Independent MPs: A Comparative Analysis of Australia and Ireland." *Parliamentary Affairs* 73 (1): 89–107.

Keman, Hans, and Ferdinand Müller-Rommel. 2012. "The Life Cycle of Party Government Across the New Europe." In *Party Government in the New Europe*, edited by Hans Keman and Ferdinand Müller-Rommel, 3–24. London/New York: Routledge.

Klüver, Heike, and Radoslaw Zubek. 2018. "Minority Governments and Legislative Reliability: Evidence From Denmark and Sweden." *Party Politics* 24 (6): 719–730.

Körösényi, András, Péter Ondré, and András Hajdú. 2017. "A Meteoric Career in Hungarian Politics." In *The Leadership Capital Index: A New Perspective on Political Leadership*, edited by Mark Bennister, Ben Worthy, and Paul't Hart, 82–100. Oxford: Oxford University Press.

Kovarek, Daniel, and Levente Littvay. 2019. "Where Did All the Environmentalism Go? 'Politics Can Be Different' (LMP) in the 2018 Hungarian Parliamentary Elections." *Environmental Politics* 28 (3): 574–582.

Kovarek, Dániel, and Gábor Soós. 2016. "Cut from the Same Cloth? A Comparative Analysis of Party Organizations in Hungary." In *Organizational Structures of Political Parties in Central and Eastern European Countries*, edited by Katarzyna Sobolewska-Myslik, Beata Kosowska-Gastol, and Piotr Borowiec, 185–208. Krakow: Jagiellonian University Press.

Lakner, Zoltán, András Pungor, Brigitta Szabó, and József Faragó. 2019. *Frontsebészet. A köztársaság utolsó kormánya*. Budapest: Telegráf Kiadó.

Lundberg, Thomas Carl. 2013. "Politics is Still An Adversarial Business: Minority Government and Mixed-member Proportional Representation in Scotland and in New Zealand." *The British Journal of Politics & International Relations* 15 (4): 609–625.

McDonnell, Duncan, and Marco Valbruzzi. 2014. "Defining and Classifying Technocrat-led and Technocratic Governments." *European Journal of Political Research* 53 (4): 654–671.

Népszabadság. 2008. "Robert Fico elutasította a magyar békejobbot." http://nol.hu/kulfold/robert_fico_elutasitotta_a_magyar_bekejobbot-311501

Népszabadság. 2009. "Bajnai: A Vatikán nem kritizált." http://nol.hu/kulfold/20091114-bajnai_a_vatikan_nem_kritizalt-428531

Nikolenyi, Csaba. 2004. "Cabinet Stability in Post-Communist Central Europe." *Party Politics* 10 (2): 123–150.

Pastorella, Giulia. 2016. "Technocratic Governments in Europe: Getting the Critique Right." *Political Studies* 64 (4): 948–965.

Ripp, Zoltán. 2010. "A Magyar Szocialista Párt 2009-ben." In *Magyarország politikai évkönyve 2009-ről*, edited by Péter Sándor and László Vass. Budapest: DKMKA.

Roberts, Andrew. 2008. "Hyperaccountability: Economic Voting in Central and Eastern Europe." *Electoral Studies* 27 (3): 533–546.

Sárközy, Tamás. 2012. *Magyarország kormányzása 1978–2012*. Budapest: Park Könyvkiadó.

Savage, Lee. 2013. "Party System Polarisation and Government Duration in Central and Eastern Europe." *West European Politics* 36 (5): 1029–1051.

Simonovits, András. 2016. "Impact of the Economic and Financial Crisis on Pension Systems in Central and Eastern Europe: Hungary." *Zeitschrift für Sozialreform* 57 (3): 287–298.

Sitter, Nick. 2011. "A magyar pártszerkezet 2010-ben: polarizáltabb, kevésbé plurális." In *Új képlet: A 2010-es választások Magyarországon*, edited by Zsolt Enyedi, Andrea Szabó, and Róbert Tardos. Budapest: DKMKA.

Somer-Topcu, Zeynep, and Laron K. Williams. 2008. "Survival of the Fittest? Cabinet Duration in Postcommunist Europe." *Comparative Politics* 40 (3): 313–329.

Stumpf, István. 2009. "Kormányválságtól a válságkormányzásig." In *Magyarország politikai évkönyve 2008-ról*, edited by Péter Sándor and László Vass. Budapest: DKMKA.

Stumpf, István. 2010. "Válságkormányzás és kormányzati stabilitás." In *Magyarország politikai évkönyve 2009-ről*, edited by Péter Sándor and László Vass. Budapest: DKMKA.

Šutaj, Štefan. 2014. "Szlovák–magyar Történelmi Párhuzamok és Konfliktusok (a Nemzeti Történelmek Közép-európai Kontextusban) Avagy a Közös Szlovák–magyar Szövegek írásáról." *Kor/ridor. Szlovák-Magyar Történeti Folyóirat* 1 (1): 9–19.

Teruel, Juan Rodríguez, and Miguel Jerez Mir. 2018. "The Selection and Deselection of Technocratic Ministers in Democratic Spain." In *Technocratic Ministers and Political Leadership in European Democracies*, edited by António Costa Pinto, Maurizio Cotta, and Pedro Tavares de Almeida, 139–171. Cham: Palgrave Macmillan.

Tóth, Csaba, and Gábor Török. 2015. *Négy választás Magyarországon. A magyar politika az elmúlt 12 évben (2002–2014)*. Budapest: Osiris.

Vegetti, Federico. 2019. "The Political Nature of Ideological Polarization: The Case of Hungary." *The ANNALS of the American Academy of Political and Social Science* 681 (1): 78–96.

Volkens, Andrea, Werner Krause, Pola Lehmann, Theres Matthieß, Nicolas Merz, Sven Regel, and Bernhard Weßels. 2019. *The Manifesto Data Collection. Manifesto Project (MRG/CMP/MARPOR). Version 2019b*. Berlin: Wissenschaftszentrum Berlin für Sozialforschung (WZB).

Zubek, Radoslaw. 2011. "Negative Agenda Control and Executive-legislative Relations in East Central Europe, 1997–2008." *The Journal of Legislative Studies* 17 (2): 172–192.

Prime ministers, presidents and ministerial selection in Lithuania

Lukas Pukelis and Mažvydas Jastramskis

ABSTRACT
In the semi-presidential system of Lithuania, a tradition to elect non-partisan presidents coexists with re-occurring conflicts between prime ministers and presidents over cabinet composition. We investigate what factors increase the probability of presidential activism in this field, i.e. when the president attempts to affect ministerial selection. We explain the outcomes of such activism by the electoral cycles and the political weakness of prime ministers and their party governments. More specifically, we argue that prime ministers are most vulnerable to presidential activism right after presidential elections and when they do not enjoy strong support in parliament. We test these hypotheses with a data set chronicling all instances of competition between the prime ministers and presidents over ministerial selection. The quantitative analysis is supplemented with qualitative insights from interviews with former cabinet members and high-level officials.

Introduction

The relationship between the president and the prime minister (PM) is at the centre of semi-presidential systems. The dualism of the executive branch allows for a wide range of theoretically expected interactions, from flexibility and power sharing to institutional conflict (Sedelius and Ekman 2010; Elgie 2011; Sedelius and Mashtaler 2013). Much of the existing research on semi-presidentialism focuses on regime stability (Beuman 2015; Elgie 2018) and democratic performance (Cheibub, Elkins, and Ginsburg 2014; Elgie 2008, 2011; Hicken and Stoll 2013; Sedelius and Linde 2018). The main argument against this system is its potential for "cohabitation" of presidents and PMs with distinct party affiliations, which may trigger intra-executive conflicts. Although dual executives sometimes lead to political stalemates or even democratic crises (Shugart and Carey 1992; Elgie 2008; Beuman 2015), most cases of semi-presidentialism avoid democracy-threatening instability (Elgie and McMenamin 2006; Elgie 2011).

Beyond regime instability, there are other instances of political conflict in semi-presidential systems that are functionally significant, such as disagreements over cabinet formation, ministerial appointments and government policies. However, as Raunio and Sedelius (2020, 1) summarise, "we still know very little about the actual functioning of day-to-day routines and coordination between the president and the prime minister".

One important area where dual executives may coordinate, compete or even go into conflict is ministerial selection. Indeed, the personal composition of the cabinet is central for the ability of the PM to organise and control the government. If the president "takes away" important ministries, she may critically affect the PM's discretion and thus threaten her survival in office.

The extant literature has not sufficiently dealt with this issue. Studies on ministerial selection in parliamentary systems have investigated the impact of intra-party diversity (Bäck, Debus, and Müller 2016), intra-party organisation (Kam et al. 2010), temporal dynamics (Fleischer and Seyfried 2015) and personal relationships (O'Malley 2006). Research on semi-presidential systems explored the overall degree of intra-executive conflict (Protsyk 2006), as well as involvement of presidents in the formation of party governments and influence over cabinet (Protsyk 2005; Schleiter and Morgan-Jones 2009; Schleiter and Morgan-Jones 2010; Bucur 2017). However, literature with a specific focus on the ministerial selection in semi-presidential systems is still scarce.

Against this background, we analyse the competition between PMs and presidents over ministerial appointments and removals. Central and Eastern Europe (CEE) is a suitable context to study such interactions. Since the transition to democracy, most of the former post-communist countries opted for a directly elected president alongside a PM appointed by parliament, which turned CEE into a laboratory of semi-presidential systems (Sedelius and Mashtaler 2013). Among these cases, Lithuania seems to be particularly interesting. Since 1998, the country has seen the constant election of independent presidents, which means that there were virtually no formal cohabitations (with an exception of Rolandas Paksas in 2003-2004) during the last two decades. Nevertheless, there have been cases of intense intra-executive conflicts over ministerial selection (Raunio and Sedelius 2020). This may be partly because the Lithuanian president has the constitutional right to approve the personal composition of cabinet. However, not all the instances of government formation and vacancies of ministerial posts have triggered intra-executive conflicts. Disputes over ministerial selection varied even under the same independent president. For example, in 1998 president Valdas Adamkus went into open conflict with PM Gediminas Vagnorius over the composition of cabinet, but did not actively intervene in the government formation after the 2008 parliamentary elections.

When do independent presidents in Lithuania interfere in ministerial selection and which factors facilitate the "victories" of either the president or the PM? To answer these questions, we first discuss the literature on the competition over ministerial selection between the president and the PM in semi-presidential systems and elaborate on hypotheses about presidential activism in this field. Second, we explain why the case of Lithuania is suitable to examine these hypotheses. The third section exhibits our data and methodological approach. Fourth, we present the empirical analysis relying on a dataset of ministerial replacements and qualitative interviews. Finally, we reflect on the implications of our results for the research on prime ministers and party governments in semi-presidential systems.

Competition over ministerial selection in semi-presidential systems

The main characteristic of semi-presidential systems is a dual executive, which consists of a popularly elected president and a PM heading a cabinet accountable to parliament

(Duverger 1980; Elgie 1999, 13). In contrast to a parliamentary system where the PM has one principal, semi-presidential systems put PMs into a situation of two principals: parliament and president (Protsyk 2006, 221). Contingent on historical context, presidential powers, partisanship of the executive branches and other factors, semi-presidential systems allow for a wide range of cooperation and conflict between the president and the PM.

Before delving more into the factors that influence this intra-executive competition in semi-presidential systems, we need to clarify our conceptual foundations. Acknowledging that interactions between the president and the PM do not often lead to high-level conflicts (political instability), we require a concept that captures intra-executive conflicts of lower intensity. Hence, we take "presidential activism" as central concept, defined by Köker (2017, 5) as "the discretionary use of formal powers by the president", which broadens the notion of intra-executive conflicts beyond the most dramatic events. According to Raunio and Sedelius (2020, 35), informal channels may also be important, leading them to conceptualise presidential activism as "presidents use of their formal powers and their attempts to influence politics through informal channels". We follow the latter definition, with a particular focus on the presidents' attempts to influence the ministerial selection (appointments or removals) as it affects the ability of a PM to organise and control her cabinet. This definition covers both the attempted presidential interventions into the ministerial selection and the occasions where such interventions lead to conflicts between the PM and the president. However, as we focus on the intra-executive competition, our definition excludes the instances where the PM and the president have agreed upon the coordination mechanisms, such as the tradition to take into consideration the opinion of president when appointing the minister of foreign affairs (Raunio and Sedelius 2019).

What factors do facilitate presidential activism and the success of this activism? In general, two categories of explanatory factors are relevant. The first category refers to the constitutional design. The potential for intra-executive competition and presidential activism is programmed into the basic structure of semi-presidential systems. When the president is elected directly, this creates a potential for "electoral separation of purpose", i.e. differing electorates of president and the parties of the governing coalition (Elgie et al. 2014, 468; Samuels and Shugart 2010, 20). This leads to an expectation of presidential activism. However, the design of Lithuanian semi-presidentialism cannot have any systematic effect on the varying degree of this activism, since it remained a constant since the restoration of independence and democratisation (see the next section).

The second category of factors refers to the political context that is favourable for a higher degree (and success) of presidential activism in the ministerial selection under a semi-presidential system. The literature highlights the following factors that may lead to higher levels of intra-executive conflicts and presidential influence over the cabinet composition. These factors are personality of president (Baylis 1996; Elgie 1999; Taras 1997), periods of cohabitation (Shugart and Carey 1992; Sedelius and Mashtaler 2013; Beuman 2015; Bucur 2017), periods of political turbulence and low societal consensus (Tavits 2009; Raunio and Sedelius 2020), weak institutionalisation of party system, weak governments (Protsyk 2006) and popularity of presidents (Raunio and Sedelius 2020). Since we analyse one country that is a relatively young democracy, we do not have much variance regarding turbulent periods and party-system institutionalisation.

Moreover, because of the tradition to elect independent presidents, formal cohabitations have been constantly absent in Lithuania (see the next section). As for the personality, it is hard to operationalise. Therefore, our analysis concentrates on the factors of weak governments and popularity of presidents.

Regarding the weak governments, we believe this factor is best conceptualised as the strength of PM's parliamentary support. If the PM does not have a solid support in the parliament, the president may be active, push his own candidates or go into a public conflict over ministerial selections by the PM, referencing the lack of PM political legitimacy: in contrast to her popular mandate. PM strength here is conceptually separate from our dependent variable (presidential activism and success in the ministerial selection), as it captures the contextual factors that lead to the position of PM in the parliament (and may affect the PM's position vis-à-vis the president).

We discern four theoretical facets of PM's support that could vary with the different governments (presidents) and may affect the success of presidential activism in the ministerial selection. The first is the institutionalisation of the PM's party: even under a relatively new party system, we expect that some parties will be less institutionalised than the others. Weak party organisation increases possibility of defections and thus reduces the support for PM within her own party. Second, unstable coalitions may also undermine the PM's backing in parliament. Third, intra-executive conflict is more likely when the PM leads a minority cabinet (Protsyk 2006). The absence of a parliamentary majority obviously reduces the strength of PM's support. Fourth, technocratic cabinets also weaken the PM: ministers in them usually do not have political allegiance and may act as independents, reducing the PMs' discretion over the cabinet.

To sum up, the power of PM directly relates to how strongly the parliament supports him or her. PMs who have solid backing in parliament can leverage this political support and use their personal authority to shield other cabinet members if they encounter any difficulties, such as conflicts with president. If a president resorts to activism with a PM who enjoys strong backing in parliament, the probability of influencing ministerial selection is low. On the other hand, if a PM lacks support within her party/coalition or faces a minority/technocratic cabinet situation, her position is weak. She will be in a less favourable position in the situations of presidential activism over ministerial selection; moreover, the weakness of PM may encourage the president to interfere.

> H1. The stronger the parliamentary support of PM, the less likely are presidents to attempt and succeed in influencing ministerial selection.

Other important contextual factors cover the electoral cycles and the popularity of PM and president. Electoral separation of purpose (Samuels and Shugart 2010) means that when the electorates of the president and the PM party differ, one may expect to gain voter sympathies by starting a conflict with another. They may achieve this by either mobilising their own voters or attracting the undecided electorate. However, there are questions regarding the timing and outcome: how do the popularity and electoral cycles contribute to the activism by presidents and probability of their success?

Presidents are usually more popular than PMs (Raunio and Sedelius 2020), but we expect a difference between newly elected and lame-duck presidents. During her first term, the president is incentivised by the prospect of re-election and this may motivate her to interfere in ministerial selection. On the other hand, re-election does not strongly motivate an outgoing president, especially in the last years of her second term. Furthermore, probably the single most powerful (and informal) tool in the presidential arsenal is to leverage her popular support to criticise the PM. A newly elected (re-elected) president is usually very popular and this may especially motivate her to be active in the very first phase of her term, immediately after (re)election.

The mechanism regarding the popularity also extends to PM. Research on the electoral cycles finds quite regular honeymoon periods: new governments enjoy an initial boost of popularity from the voters for several months (Green and Jennings 2017). Even though voters usually punish the governments at the polls in the CEE region and the probability of getting re-elected is rather weak (Roberts 2008; Jastramskis et al. 2018), PMs here also start with quite high levels of support. A "fresh" PM with (still) undiminished popular support will be stronger than an office-weary PM. In this situation, PMs may have the power to effectively react to presidential interference and prevail. Therefore, we expect that if president resorts to activism over ministerial selection, the possibility of her success is diminished in the situation of newly elected PM.

H2a. Newly elected presidents are more likely to be active and win over incumbent prime ministers.

H2b. Newly elected PMs are more likely to win over incumbent presidents.

The case of Lithuania

In 1992, the newly adopted Constitution of Lithuania established the institution of a directly elected president alongside the prime minister. The president nominates the PM for the approval of *Seimas* (parliament), but the removal of cabinet is the prerogative of parliament. Overall, the Lithuanian president enjoys medium powers if compared to other semi-presidential systems in Europe (Sedelius 2006; Elgie et al. 2014; Raunio and Sedelius 2020). The most recent index of presidential power places the country higher than the regional average (Andrews and Bairett 2019).

Two institutional features of Lithuanian semi-presidentialism are particular relevant for our analysis. First, the president's choice of PM is effectively restricted by the preferences of the governing coalition in parliament, making this power a mere formality (Krupavičius 2008). Second, the president has to approve the personal composition of cabinet. Thus, even though president's hands are bound in selecting the PM, she can attempt to affect ministerial selection and thus "intrude" into the PM's discretion. Thus, the Lithuanian case is quite favourable for a study of presidential activism in the field of ministerial selection.

In general, non-concurrent parliamentary and presidential elections are also conducive to intra-executive competition as they may lead to divergent partisan affiliations of presidents and PMs. In this regard, however, Lithuania is a peculiar case. Article 83 of the Constitution stipulates that elected presidents have to suspend activities in political parties. Furthermore, Lithuanian voters tend to elect independent presidents. This creates a context in which formal cohabitations are not likely to emerge. On the other hand, periods of truly unified government (that strengthen the presidential influence over cabinet composition in other cases: [Bucur 2017]), are also absent in Lithuania. Brazauskas was the last true partisan president: voters elected him in 1993 as a leader of ex-communist Lithuanian Democratic Labour Party. Partly due to the non-partisanship of Lithuanian presidents, Raunio and Sedelius (2020, 64) find that "power-sharing with low levels of conflict has characterised the president–prime minister relationship for the most part". Indeed, especially regarding the legislation and foreign affairs, cooperation or at least non-interference is the usual *modus operandi* in the intra-executive relations. However, Raunio and Sedelius (2020) also observe that all presidents had open conflicts with PMs regarding the cabinet composition. Moreover, some presidents even managed to remove PMs from power: Algirdas M. Brazauskas (vs. Mykolas Šleževičius in 1995; both from the same party) and non-partisan president Valdas Adamkus (vs. conservative Gediminas Vagnorius in 1998) won their battles irrespective of their partisanship. Moreover, as exemplified by our data (see Table 1), presidential activism in Lithuania varies even under one and the same president. This leads us to ask what circumstances prompt (successful) presidential activism.

Before analysing this question empirically, we need to comment on the possibility of "hidden partisanship". Although not being formal party members, Lithuanian presidents may have some partisan inclinations. Some of them even enjoyed support of particular parties in the elections, like Adamkus by centrists in 1998 or Dalia Grybauskaitė by the conservatives and liberals in 2009 and 2014. However, such (suspected) preferences do not seem to have systematically affected the activism of presidents in the field of ministerial selection. First, as mentioned before, all presidents went into conflicts with some PMs. Second, as descriptive statistics indicate (see Table 2), even in the period when president Grybauskaitė faced a government coalition of conservatives and liberals (2009-2012), her level of activism was relatively high.

Data and methods

The ensuing empirical analysis includes ten Lithuanian cabinets during the tenures of two presidents: Valdas Adamkus and Dalia Grybauskaitė (see Table 1). Our choice to focus on these cases and exclude the presidencies of Brazauskas and Nausėda was mainly prompted by the availability of data. Nausėda assumed the presidency in mid-2019 and there simply is not enough data on his relationship with the PMs yet. Meanwhile, even though Brazauskas presidency would have been an interesting case (he was first and, so far, the only partisan president), our analysis strongly relies on the searchable full-text media archives to look up cases of presidential activism. For most of the daily newspapers and web portals in Lithuania these archives go back to around 1997, which roughly corresponds to the start of Adamkus presidency (Table 1).

We employ a mixed-method approach, by first using quantitative data to illustrate the broad patterns. This dataset covers the period from 1998 to 2019 and was assembled from three main sources: news media, administrative records, and insider interviews. The unit of analysis is a single cabinet membership, i.e. one ministerial tenure. Overall, the dataset includes 245 memberships in ten different cabinets.

The key concept of presidential activism is covered by two variables in our dataset. The first is "presence of presidential activism", which is a dummy variable denoting whether the president used her influence through formal or informal channels to influence the appointment or dismissal of a particular minister. The second variable, "success of

Table 1. Cabinets in Lithuania under the presidencies of Valdas Adamkus (1998–2009) and Dalia Grybauskaitė (2009–2019).

Cabinet	Date in	Date out	PM duration[b]	Cabinet duration[b]	Party composition[c]	Cabinet type[d]	President
Vagnorius	1996-11-28	1999-05-04	887	887	**TS-LK**, LKDP, LCS	SUR	Adamkus
Paksas (I)	1999-05-18	1999-10-27	162	162	**TS-LK**, LKDP, LCS	SUR	Adamkus
Kubilius (I)	1999-11-3	2000-10-26	358	358	**TS-LK**, LKDP, LCS	SUR	Adamkus
Paksas (II)	2000-10-26	2001-06-20	237	237	**LLiS**, NS	MIN	Adamlus
Brazauskas (I)	2001-07-03	2004-12-14	1260	1794	**LSDP**, NS	SUR	Adamkus
Brazauskas (II)	2004-12-14	2006-06-01	534	1794	DP, **LSDP**, LVLS, NS	MWC	Adamkus
Kirkilas	2006-07-04	2008-12-09	889	889	**LSDP**, LVLS, LiCS, PDP	MIN	Adamkus
Kubilius (II)	2008-12-09	2012-12-13	1465	1465	**TS-LK**, TPP, LRLS, LiCS	MWC	Grybauskaitė
Butkevičius	2012-12-13	2016-12-13	1461	1461	**LSDP**, DP, LLRA, TT-LDP	SUR	Grybauskaitė
Skvernelis[a]	2016-12-13	2019-07-12	941	941	**LZVS**, LSDP	MWC	Grybauskaitė

Sources: Döring and Manow (2012), Zarate (2019).
[a]Since the term of PM Skvernelis was not completed at the time of writing, the end date of Grybauskaitė presidential term is used as end date of the cabinet, indicating the duration of the overlap between the terms of PM Skvernelis and president Grybauskaitė.
[b]The horizontal lines demarcate parliamentary terms. Office duration in days.
[c]Party of PM marked in bold; parties ordered by parliamentary size.
[d]MIN-minority; MWC-minimal winning coalition; SUR-surplus.

presidential activism", denotes whether the president managed to successfully affect ministerial selection/deselection. Overall, we have identified 30 instances of presidential activism and 24 presidential "wins".

In the dataset, we also provide links to the relevant media articles next to each instance of presidential activism as well as a brief commentary on what had transpired, so that the data used in our analysis are replicable to the maximum possible extent. We performed a media analysis using the searchable internet archives of popular Lithuanian daily and weekly newspapers, as well as internet portals that we considered most useful for this research: "delfi.lt", "15min.lt", "lrytas.lt", "vz.lt", "tv3.lt", "alfa.lt" and "ve.lt". These outlets have been active for the major part of the investigation period and had a functionality enabling the full-text search of their archive material.

In our quantitative analysis, we concentrate on bivariate statistics – a necessity dictated by the nature of the data and the limited size of the dataset. This analysis is supplemented with insights from insider interviews to provide a more detailed and rich narrative. For these interviews, we targeted high-profile officials familiar with intra-executive conflicts, including former ministers and PMs. In total, we have individually interviewed five such insiders.

Results

In this section, we present the results of our analysis. Some quotes from the qualitative interviews include triangle brackets ("< ... >") symbols to mark omissions of sensitive

PM parliamentary support

Our first hypothesis is that presidents are less likely to engage and succeed in ministerial selection if a PM commands a strong and unified support in parliament. To test this hypothesis we have created a "PM strength score" which can range from zero to four and corresponds to the four factors that affect the PM strength discussed in the theory section: minority cabinet, technocratic cabinet, unstable coalition, and party disunity. The score is calculated as follows: the highest score is four – it means that no factors that weaken a PM were present in that cabinet. For each of the conditions present, we subtract one from the ideal score. If all four factors are present together in a single cabinet, then the PM strength score would be zero.

We coded cabinets that did not have a majority in parliament as minority cabinets. We define technocratic cabinets as Cabinets where more than 40 percent of ministers were not members of a governing party. Cabinets, for which either our interviewees or media sources indicated that one or more coalition partners voted in an unpredictable or unreliable manner, were coded as unstable coalitions. Finally, cabinets where the interviewees indicated that the PM did not have full support of his party were coded as a case of party disunity. Each cabinet was given a score based on these four components ranging from 0 – weak PM to 4 – strong PM. Table 2 contains a breakdown of the PM strength scores and frequency of presidential activism instances by cabinet (Table 2).

The PM strength score is negatively, strongly and significantly correlated with the frequency of presidential activism (*Pearson-r* = −0.69, *p* = 0.03). Another way to look at this is to compare the mean PM strength scores for observations (i.e. individual ministerial tenures) when presidential activism did not occur and for those observations where it did. Student's *T*-test results demonstrate that the PMs were significantly weaker in instances when the presidential activism occurred (Table 3).

We found no significant difference in success rates of presidential activism depending on PM strength. This most likely occurs because in this case, the population is limited to

Table 2. PM weakness score and instances of presidential activism by cabinet.

PM	Presidential activism instances	Presidential "wins"	PM strength score	Minority cabinet	Technocratic cabinet	Unstable coalition	Party Disunity
Skvernelis	7	7	1	0	1	1	1
Butkevicius	8	5	2	0	0	1	1
Kubilius II	6	4	3	0	0	1	0
Kirkilas	2	2	2	1	0	1	0
Brazauskas II	1	1	3	0	0	1	0
Brazauskas I	0	0	4	0	0	0	0
Paksas II	2	2	2	0	0	1	1
Kubilius I	0	0	4	0	0	0	0
Paksas I	2	1	3	0	0	0	1
Vagnorius	2	2	3	0	0	0	1

Source: Authors' calculations.

PRIME MINISTERS AND PARTY GOVERNMENTS IN CENTRAL AND EASTERN EUROPE

Table 3. PM strength score and presidential interventions.

Combined N = 245	Presidential activism	No Presidential Activism
N	30	215
Mean PM strength score (SD)	1.13 (0.14)	2.73 (0.07)
p value of T-test	<0.0001	

Source: Authors' calculations.

the 30 cases of presidential activism and we are comparing a group of 24 "wins" to the group of 6 loses. Due to the small size of these groups the differences become statistically insignificant. However, the high share of presidential wins in itself is consistent with our hypothesis.

The findings of the quantitative analysis were also supported by the interviews. All interviewees, regardless of their affiliation to the respective presidential or PM office indicated that though in the popular opinion the president is perceived as the PM's superior, in practice the president is also dependent on PM to advance her domestic agenda. Therefore, the president has the informal power to successfully intervene into the ministerial selection. However, she also has to pick the battles carefully.

In Lithuania, during presidential elections candidates campaign not only on the issues of foreign and security policy, but also raise certain domestic policy issues and upon election they are expected to tackle these issues. While the presidents have the power to initiate legislation, they have to rely on the PM to get their bills through the parliament. For instance, bringing more transparency to domestic politics was a big part of Grybauskaitė's platform. One of the central pieces of this agenda was bill banning business entities from financially supporting political parties. The president initiated the bill but relied on the support from the PM (Kubilius) to get it adopted.

Furthermore, presidents' face additional difficulties because the presidential office has no legal power to summon desired documents or experts/witnesses from the executive branch and no mechanisms exist that can constantly keep the presidential office informed of what is happening in the ministries. Instead, the presidential office has to rely on the good will of the cabinet to provide relevant information or to attend the meetings with the presidential staff.

The respondents agreed that a PM backed by a coherent parliamentary majority is in a more powerful position than a president and can easily dismiss any advances from the president. As one former PM put it:

> If you have 80 MPs backing you [71 MPs are enough for majority in Seimas] then you can say "Thanks, but I decline" to whatever the president is trying to suggest, because then there is nothing he can do.

However, these instances are rather rare and often PMs found themselves in a weak position. Several interviewees pointed out that the strength of the PM's position depends on various factors. One of them, of course, is the numeric size of the governing coalition. However, other factors were also considered important: external crises that quickly erode the public support for the PM, internal strife in the party and lack of internal backing for the PM, technocratic nature of the cabinet (where ministers do not have the full backing of a party behind them) and weak institutionalisation of parties in the coalition.

Some interviewees drew attention to the Butkevičius cabinet, which on the outset commanded a strong majority in parliament. However, many instances of presidential activism occurred during its tenure (see Table 2). Interviewees suggested that this occurred because Butkevičius did not have the full support from his own party and the party disunity created grounds for presidential activism.

Meanwhile, a former PM from a different cabinet recalled a situation when two ministers, a non-partisan technocrat and a politician strongly backed by one of the coalition partners, faced criticism from the president who urged for the ministers to step down. However, out of the two, only the technocrat was dismissed. The PM indicated that in such situation he had no means to defend a minister who had no backing from the party against the criticism from the president.

In other words, lacking support from government parties made a cabinet member more vulnerable and created opportunities for presidential activism. Cohesive parties can extend their full backing to the PM and her cabinet, thus significantly strengthening PM's position. On the other hand, weakly institutionalised parties tend to lack internal cohesion. Moreover, they may struggle in finding suitable candidates for the cabinet positions after winning the parliamentary elections. In such cases, the PM's position is weak, and this weakness "invites" activism from the president.

Some of our interviewees pointed out that weaker PMs could even reach out to the president and actively seek presidential intervention into the process of ministerial selection. Based on the interview data, up to a half of the Skvernelis cabinet was assembled from the candidates initially put forward by the president. The PM and the party behind him simply did not have enough experienced members to govern and occupy cabinet positions. Therefore, the president had an opportunity to put forward candidacies and actively participate in the cabinet formation.

We see this as one of the main contributions of our research to the theory of PM–President relations in semi-presidential systems. Current approaches depict presidential activism in mostly negative terms and see that as a disruptive or destabilising factor. Meanwhile, our evidence demonstrates that presidential activism can be a positive influence and help to stave off the worst effects of party system instability and electoral volatility.

Finally, PM strength appears to be tied to the institutionalisation of her party. Stronger institutionalised parties have more capable cadre to fill the cabinet positions. They are more cohesive and thus less dependent on the president for help. This shrinks the room for presidential activism. In contrast, weakly institutionalised parties have a more difficult time to find suitable people for governing positions and lack internal cohesion to function smoothly. All this makes them more reliant on the president to intervene.

The evidence outlined above leads us to conclude that our first hypothesis is supported. The broad trends from the quantitative data and the expert interviews confirm that presidential activism increases when the PM is considered to have weak parliamentary support. This can be caused by the fact that the PM does not command a majority in the Seimas but also because of many other reasons, such as unreliable coalition partners, the technocratic nature of the cabinet or the lack of support from the PM's own party.

Overall, presidential activism in about 80 percent of the cases results in a presidential "win". We did not find any significant differences in presidential "win" rates when the PM is strongly backed or not. However, this pattern is consistent with our hypothesis that presidents are likely to engage and succeed in presidential activism when the PM is not strongly backed in parliament, as we demonstrate that presidents are indeed more likely to engage in activism against weak PMs and in most cases this activism produces a "win".

Electoral cycles

According to our second hypothesis, presidential activism is influenced by electoral cycles.[1] We have plotted the frequency of presidential activism over time and alongside parliamentary and presidential elections (Figure 1). Both figures show that parliamentary and presidential elections are usually followed by an uptick of presidential activism. This is consistent with Hypothesis 2a. We found no significant difference in the success of presidential activism comparing the first year after parliamentary election when a new PM was in office and other time periods. However, this is mostly due to the small sample size (Figures 1 and 2).

The interviewees were broadly in agreement that electoral cycles matter for the general dynamics of the PM-presidential competition over the cabinet composition. For instance, newly elected presidents often demanded the replacement of certain ministers for no other reason than demonstrating to the public that they are "being tough on the PM". In fact, a former PM indicated that he had *ex ante* expected that the newly elected president would ask to replace a minister, so when the request came he was not at all surprised to receive it. Such testimony nicely serves to illustrate the pattern consistent with our Hypothesis 2a.

In contrast, outgoing presidents were perceived as being not so powerful or capable to intervene in cabinet affairs. Interviewed insiders indicated that in the final year of the

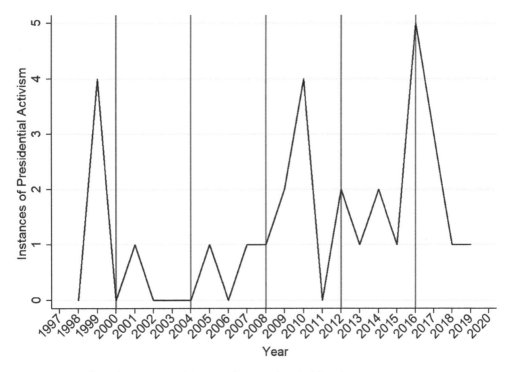

Figure 1. Presidential activism and Seimas elections (vertical lines).

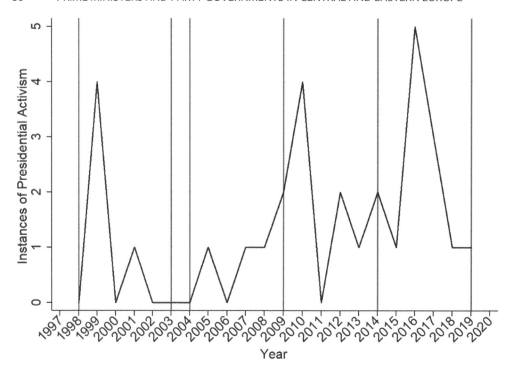

Figure 2. Presidential activism and presidential elections (vertical lines).

president's term, the focus lied on the upcoming presidential election and the capacity of the president to leverage the popular opinion and to exert her will on the PM greatly diminishes.

However, the expert consensus only covers the presidential election cycle. For the Seimas election cycle and the PM life cycle (H2b), their opinions differed. Some experts contended that newly appointed PMs can leverage their fresh mandate and stave off presidential advances. One former PM indicated that immediately after the election the cabinet has positive momentum and the greatest capacity to overcome any obstacle, which then gradually diminishes throughout the term. However, other experts pointed out that it is precisely just after taking PM office that new cabinets are most vulnerable to presidential advances. More specifically, newly formed cabinet might lack experience of working together and be less cohesive, which opens up opportunities for the president.

Overall, there is enough quantitative and qualitative evidence to demonstrate that the presidential election cycle has a significant effect on presidential activism. Newly elected presidents seek to bolster their public image and seek to be perceived as "tough" on the PM (H2a). However, we did not find enough support that newly appointed PMs are better equipped to resist the president (H2b). Rather, presidential activism increases in frequency after parliamentary elections when a new PM is appointed. This shows that presidents see these occasions as favourable for activism. Though we did not find statistically significant differences in the success rates of presidential activism between newly appointed and seasoned PMs, the number of instances when presidential activism was not successful is so small that the existing differences are not statistically significant.

Conclusion

Semi-presidentialism is the most frequent regime type in Central and Eastern Europe. Nevertheless, we still know little about how these regimes function day-to-day and how the interactions between the PM and the president unfold. We sought to shed more light on this issue, by analysing how the presidents intervene into the ministerial selection process in Lithuania. Between 1998 and 2019, our research found 30 instances of presidential activism, when a president sought to influence who is appointed to or is dismissed from cabinet. In 80 percent or 24 cases, the presidents have been successful.

Based on the data we gathered from the media and insider interviews, we can draw the following conclusions. First, presidents actively engage with the ministerial selection not only during the cabinet formation phase, but also throughout the whole life cycle of the cabinet. Presidents can use their informal powers to pressure the PM to dismiss or veto a certain minister. Thus, presidents can "insert" themselves into the cabinet. That in turn constrains the PM's ability to manage their cabinet and influence policy.

We found evidence that presidential activism is related to the PM's position in the parliament. Weaker PMs do not have a full capacity to resist the president, which provides an opportunity for presidential activism. This is quite natural and well established. However, we show that this hypothesis also works in a previously unexplored context of independent presidents in CEE. Our analysis reveals that intra-executive competition and signs of cohabitation occur even if a president is not affiliated with any political party. Moreover, differently from research on France (Bucur 2017), we find that presidential influence over the cabinet (ministerial selection) can be strong even when a unified government is not possible: i.e. under independent presidents.

Regarding the electoral cycle, we observed a quite clear pattern that newly elected presidents tend to be the most active. In the period following their election, presidents seek to make use of the high levels of popular support and present themselves as being "tough on the PM". We also observed an uptick of presidential activism during the formation of post-electoral cabinets.

These findings may come as unsurprising for the CEE region, where weak parties and fluid party systems naturally open up avenues for the presidential activism. However, our analysis adds a novelty: presidential activism is not always unwelcomed by the parties. Rather, it may help weaker PMs, especially those from the new and/or underdeveloped parties, to fill-in the vacant cabinet positions with capable people. This was especially true for the Skvernelis cabinet, when the party that won the election did not have enough cadre to fill the cabinet positions. Activism of independent president Grybauskaitė increased in this case, because a "fresh" prime minister needed help. We believe this insight is one of the main theoretical contributions of this paper. Future research could further explore this, applying our framework in a broader comparative setting.

Our analysis raises questions about the effects of presidential activism for the future research. Does it work to stabilise the political system against the worst effects of electoral volatility and party system fluidity? Alternatively, is it an executive overreach that infringes upon the mandate of the parliament as the main principal of the cabinet? Another avenue of research could focus exclusively on how the PMs perceive presidential activism: under what circumstances do they welcome and shun it.

Note

1. In Lithuania, the support for cabinets usually follows a stable pattern – it is high right after the cabinet formation and then diminishes slowly. Hence, by looking at the impact of the electoral cycles, we also indirectly take into account the popularity of the PM. We also ran correlations between the instances of presidential activism and the support for the president and the PM from the public opinion polls. We found some negative correlation between the support for the PM and presidential activism and some positive correlation between the support for the president and presidential activism, but none of these were statistically significant.

Disclosure statement

No potential conflict of interest was reported by the author(s).

References

Andrews, J. T., and R. L. Bairett. 2019. "Measuring Executive Power." Working Paper.

Baylis, T. 1996. "Presidents Versus Prime Ministers: Shaping the Executive Authority in Eastern Europe." *World Politics* 48 (3): 297–323.

Bäck, H., M. Debus, and W. C. Müller. 2016. "Intra-party Diversity and Ministerial Selection in Coalition Governments." *Public Choice* 166 (3-4): 355–378.

Beuman, L. M. 2015. "Cohabitation in New Post-Conflict Democracies: The Case of Timor-Leste." *Parliamentary Affairs* 68 (3): 453–475.

Bucur, C. 2017. "Cabinet Ministers Under Competing Pressures: Presidents, Prime Ministers, and Political Parties in Semi-Presidential Systems." *Comparative European Politics* 15: 180–203.

Cheibub, J. A., Z. Elkins, and T. Ginsburg. 2014. "Beyond Presidentialism and Parliamentarism." *British Journal of Political Science* 44 (3): 515–544.

Döring, H., and P. Manow. 2012. "Parliament and Government Composition Database (ParlGov)." *An Infrastructure for Empirical Information on Parties, Elections and Governments in Modern Democracies*. Version, 12(10).

Duverger, M. 1980. "A New Political System Model: Semi-Presidential Government." *European Journal of Political Research* 8 (2): 165–187.

Elgie, R. 1999. "The Politics of Semi-Presidentialism." In *Semi-Presidentialism in Europe*, edited by R. Elgie, 1–21. Oxford: Oxford University Press.

Elgie, R. 2008. "The Perils of Semi-Presidentialism. Are They Exaggerated?" *Democratization* 15 (1): 49–66.

Elgie, R. 2011. "Semi-Presidentialism: An Increasingly Common Constitutional Choice." In *Semi-Presidentialism and Democracy*, edited by R. Elgie, S. Moestrup, and Y. Wu, 1–20. New York: Palgrave Macmillan.

Elgie, R. 2018. *Political Leadership: A Pragmatic Institutionalist Approach*. London: Palgrave Macmillan.

Elgie, R., C. Bucur, B. Dolez, and A. Laurent. 2014. "Proximity, Candidates, and Presidential Power: How Directly Elected Presidents Shape the Legislative Party System." *Political Research Quarterly* 67 (3): 467–477.

Elgie, R., and I. McMenamin. 2006. "Divided Executives and Democratisation". *Working Papers in International Studies*. Centre for International Studies, Dublin City University.

Fleischer, J., and M. Seyfried. 2015. "Drawing from the Bargaining Pool: Determinants of Ministerial Selection in Germany." *Party Politics* 21 (4): 503–514.

Green, J., and W. Jennings. 2017. *The Politics of Competence: Parties, Public Opinion and Voters.* Cambridge: Cambridge University Press.

Hicken, A., and H. Stoll. 2013. "Are All Presidents Created Equal? Presidential Powers and the Shadow of Presidential Elections." *Comparative Political Studies* 46 (3): 291–319.

Jastramskis, Mažvydas, Jūratė Kavaliauskaitė, Vaidas Morkevičius, Ieva-Petronytė Urbonavičienė, and Ainė Ramonaitė. 2018. *Ar Galime Prognozuoti Seimo Rinkimus? Trijų Kūnų Problema Lietuvos Politikoje.* Vilnius: Vilnius University Press.

Kam, C., W. T. Bianco, I. Sened, and R. Smyth. 2010. "Ministerial Selection and Intraparty Organization in the Contemporary British Parliament." *American Political Science Review* 104 (2): 289–306.

Köker, P. 2017. *Presidential Activism and Veto Power in Central and Eastern Europe.* Cham: Palgrave Macmillan.

Krupavičius, A. 2008. ""Semi-Presidentialism in Lithuania: Origins, Development and Challenges"." In *Semi-presidentialism in Central and Eastern Europe*, edited by R. Elgie, and S. Moestrup, 65–84. Manchester: Manchester University Press.

O'Malley, E. 2006. "Ministerial Selection in Ireland: Limited Choice in a Political Village." *Irish Political Studies* 21 (3): 319–336.

Protsyk, O. 2005. "Prime Ministers' Identity in Semi-Presidential Regimes: Constitutional Norms and Cabinet Formation Outcomes." *European Journal of Political Research* 44 (5): 721–748.

Protsyk, O. 2006. "Intra-executive Competition Between President and Prime Minister: Patterns of Institutional Conflict and Cooperation Under Semi-Presidentialism." *Political Studies* 54 (2): 219–244.

Raunio, T., and T. Sedelius. 2019. "Shifting Power-Centres of Semi-Presidentialism: Exploring Executive Coordination in Lithuania." *Government and Opposition* 54 (4): 637–660.

Raunio, T., and T. Sedelius. 2020. *Semi-Presidential Policy-Making in Europe: Executive Coordination and Political Leadership.* Cham: Palgrave Macmillan.

Roberts, A. 2008. "Hyperaccountability: Economic Voting in Central and Eastern Europe." *Electoral Studies* 27 (3): 533–546.

Samuels, D. J., and M. S. Shugart. 2010. *Presidents, Parties, and Prime Ministers: How the Separation of Powers Affects Party Organization and Behavior.* Cambridge: Cambridge University Press.

Schleiter, P., and E. Morgan-Jones. 2009. "Party Government in Europe? Parliamentary and Semi-Presidential Democracies Compared." *European Journal of Political Research* 48 (5): 665–693.

Schleiter, P., and E. Morgan-Jones. 2010. "Who's in Charge? Presidents, Assemblies, and the Political Control of Semipresidential Cabinets." *Comparative Political Studies* 43 (11): 1415–1441.

Sedelius, T. 2006. *The Tug-of-War Between Presidents and Prime Ministers: Semi- Presidentialism in Central and Eastern Europe.* Örebro: Örebro Studies in Political Science 15.

Sedelius, T., and J. Ekman. 2010. "Intra-Executive Conflict and Cabinet Instability: Effects of Semi-Presidentialism in Central and Eastern Europe." *Government and Opposition* 45 (4): 505–530.

Sedelius, T., and J. Linde. 2018. "Unravelling Semi-Presidentialism: Democracy and Government Performance in Four Distinct Regime Types." *Democratization* 25 (1): 136–157.

Sedelius, T., and O. Mashtaler. 2013. "Two Decades of Semi-Presidentialism: Issues of Intra-Executive Conflict in Central and Eastern Europe 1991–2011." *East European Politics* 29 (2): 109–134.

Shugart, M. S., and J. M. Carey. 1992. *Presidents and Assemblies. Constitutional Design and Electoral Dynamics.* Cambridge: Cambridge University Press.

Taras, R. 1997. *Post-Communist Presidents.* Cambridge: Cambridge University Press.

Tavits, M. 2009. *Presidents with Prime Ministers: Do Direct Elections Matter?* Oxford: Oxford University Press.

Zarate, R. O. 2019. "Leaders of Lithuania." http://zarate.eu/lithuania.htm.

Puppets of the president? Prime ministers in post-communist Romania

Laurențiu Ștefan [ID]

ABSTRACT

With sixteen Prime Ministers (PMs) in thirty years, Romania seems to fit well in the Central and Eastern European pattern of countries with "weak" heads of party governments. This article aims at contributing to the extant literature by focusing on the relationship between presidents and PMs in the Romanian context. In doing so, it challenges the general assumption that in semi-presidential systems heads of state predominate over heads of government. The empirical analysis of all Romanian chief executives since 1989 reveals that the actual power of presidents over PMs largely depends on their political convergence with the parliamentary majority.

Introduction

Over the last thirty years, Romania had sixteen Prime Ministers (PMs) who served under four different presidents. These heads of government had both short and long tenures. Tensions between presidents and PMs affected the duration of prime-ministerial tenure. For instance, a conflict between President Ion Iliescu and PM Petre Roman in September 1991 led to the dismissal of the latter. The confrontation between President Emil Constantinescu and PM Radu Vasile had the same outcome at the end of 1999. In contrast, President Traian Basescu's favoured PMs, Emil Boc and Mihai Razvan Ungureanu, have both seen their terms interrupted or ended by motions of non-confidence while Basescu himself was impeached twice by government coalitions of parties led by the then incumbent PMs. Finally, President Klaus Iohannis was forced to accept heads of government from the other side of the political spectrum.

This anecdotal evidence seems to conflict with the existing view on semi-presidentialism in Central and Eastern Europe (CEE) that PMs are generally weak because of powerful presidents (Baylis 2007), and that the former are under the tight control of the latter. In other words, PMs are considered puppets in the hands of the master puppeteer – the president. This article investigates the relationship between Romanian presidents and PMs in a systematic way. More specifically, it seeks to explore the factors that make one powerful and another one weak – or vice versa. In doing so, it argues that the predominance of the president over the PM largely depends on her political alignment with the parties that control the parliamentary majority. Vice versa, presidential power is dramatically reduced when the parliamentary majority is hostile to the president. In this case, a PM that is politically endorsed by the president may easily fall prey to a motion of non-confidence, while a PM that has the support of the parliamentary majority may survive a hostile president.

The next section introduces these theoretical considerations in more detail. This is followed by a description of the Romanian semi-presidential system and an overview of presidents, PMs and cabinets in post-communist Romania. The main section investigates the relationship between the four presidents and the respective PMs since 1989. The conclusion wraps up the empirical findings and discusses their implications.

The predominance of presidents over prime ministers in semi-presidential systems

The emergence of party governments in the new democracies of CEE prompted comparisons with consolidated democracies in Western Europe. Scholars from both parts of Europe have been quick to discover that tenures of cabinets and PMs are shorter in the region than in the West (Baylis 2007; Blondel and Müller-Rommel 2001; Protsyk 2005; Sedelius and Ekman 2010). Empirical studies led these scholars to the conclusion that "the typical East European prime minister in the post-communist period has rarely remained in office long enough to solidify his authority, much less to dominate his nations' politics" (Baylis 2007, 82). PMs in CEE are thus considered "weak" whereas their Western counterparts are "strong figures" (ibid.).

Baylis (2007, 96) contends that the main cause for prime-ministerial weakness in CEE is the "volatility" of post-communist party systems. At the same time, state presidents may have an impact on the fate of PMs: "In Eastern Europe, the position of presidents has been stronger, often leading to open conflicts which have weakened the prime minister's authority" (Baylis 2007, 89). This is more the case in semi-presidential systems than in parliamentary ones. Sedelius and Ekman (2010) identify "intra-executive conflicts" as the main reason for "cabinet instability" (Sedelius and Ekman 2010, 505–510). Like Baylis (2007), they take cabinet duration as the main measure for prime-ministerial weakness. One of their theoretical underpinnings is that "the president can exert strong influence on the cabinet" even if the formal "authority to dismiss the cabinet rests exclusively with the parliamentary majority" (Sedelius and Ekman 2010, 511).

According to the extant literature, the major power the president has over the PM in semi-presidential systems derives from her constitutional prerogative to nominate the PM (Samuels and Shugart 2010, 29). However, when it comes to the survival of PM, most scholars converge in giving the parliament the key role in her "deselection" (Sedelius and Ekman 2010, 511). But although the president does not have formal competencies in this process, she may nevertheless have the authority to influence if not determine the PM's fate (Baylis 2007, 89–90; Sedelius and Ekman 2010, 511). In particular, she may lean on her popular mandate and use her greater popularity to severely criticise the government, which "may ultimately force the prime minister out of office despite the fact that the president lacks formal dismissal powers" (Sedelius and Ekman 2010, 511). Moreover, "informal partisan power" would give the president "extra-constitutional powers to censor the cabinet" (Sedelius and Ekman 2010, 512).

Against this background, popularly elected presidents in CEE may often be "tempted to interpret the relationship with the cabinet as a relationship between principal and agent" (Protsyk 2005, 135). This is "one enduring source of tension between the president and the prime minister" (Protsyk 2005, 137). However, there are also instances when the coexistence of powerful presidents and PMs is less problematic, for example when the two "belong to the same majority" or in cases of "technocratic cabinets" (Protsyk 2005, 142).

This article builds on the mentioned literature to explore the power of the president over the PM in the Romanian context. Romanian presidents traditionally exert significant influence over the PMs, not only during the nomination process, but also on the latter's survival in office. Oleh Protsyk and other scholars hinted to the fact that the power of presidents over the PMs varies, but did not provide any systematic analysis of this variation and the circumstances that foster or hinder the predominance of the president over the PM. This article sets out to address this issue by investigating the factors that lead to more or less influence of the presidents over PMs.

In the following, the predominance of the president is explored with regard to the selection *and* the survival of the PM. The main argument is that the powers to nominate the PM and to maintain her in office depend largely on the degree of "political convergence" between the president and the parties that control the parliamentary majority. This factor has the greatest impact on the powers of the president to impose her will on the PM. The political convergence between the president and the parliamentary majority is usually indicated by whether the president originated from one of the parties composing the parliamentary majority. From this perspective, relevant cases may fall in three different categories.

Strong convergence between president and parliamentary majority exists when the president belongs or belonged to the senior party of the parliamentary majority and retains a strong position within this party. The power of the president over the PM is expected to be significant when this partisan convergence is strong. Given her authority inside the party, the president can easily impose the candidate of her choice and keep a tight control over the PM, the cabinet and even the parliamentary majority.

The category of *weak convergence* is characterised by two features. First, both the parliamentary majority and the government are based on a coalition of parties. Second, the president has a strong connection with one (not necessarily the senior) coalition party, but her party does not have a full grip on the parliamentary majority, e.g. in the case of minority cabinets. In this category, the power of the president is still significant, but no longer absolute and greatly restricted by other political actors that have a vetting power. These might be other coalition parties and/or parties supporting a minority government. Therefore, while still having the upper hand, the president has to share the responsibility of nominating the PM and of dismissing her (if this becomes an option) with other parliamentary parties.

There is *no convergence* between the president and the parties of the parliamentary majority when the president has links to one of the opposition parties, a situation known as "cohabitation". Non-concurrent legislative and presidential elections increase the chances of cohabitation in the dual executive (Elgie 2010, 38). In this case, the presidential power to nominate the PM and to determine her survival in office are drastically reduced. In the aftermath of legislative elections, the incumbent president is practically compelled to accept the candidate for PM proposed by the parties that control the parliamentary majority. Similarly, in the aftermath of presidential elections, the newly elected president may face a PM and a parliamentary majority that are already in place – and are usually hostile to her.

The relationship between president and PM is not static: an initial good relationship between the two may turn to a conflictual one. At the same time, the power of the president over one PM may vary over time. Variation comes from the fact that changes in the composition and the political orientation of the parliamentary majority may occur during a single legislative term. A situation of convergence may turn into one of no convergence if one or more governing parties join the opposition parties. Within-term changes of the parliamentary majority impact the intra-executive relationship in two possible ways. First, a PM supported by the president may be taken down by a motion of non-confidence in parliament. Second, a PM whom the president wants to dismiss may find unexpected support from the new parliamentary majority.

All these combinations, possibilities and even the dynamic relationship between one president and one prime minister can be explained by looking at the degree of political convergence between the president and the parliamentary majority: *The more convergent is the president with the parliamentary majority, the greater her power over the nomination and survival of the PM.*

I argue that this conceptual and analytical framework is more sophisticated and cannot be reduced to the simple application of the concept of "cohabitation" or "semi-presidentialism à la française" (Marrani 2009, etc.) to Central and East European countries. Indeed, one may use the CEE countries as a "laboratory" for models of interactions between the president and the prime minister that are common in Western Europe. However, there is now widespread agreement that political life in the CEE countries has been shaped by factors that were less important or non-existent in the West. One has also to take into account that there are more types of semi-presidentialism, while acknowledging at the same time that the French type of semi-presidentialism is the most famous one, and the one who imposed the term "cohabitation".

There are at least two factors in France that are not at work in countries with semi-presidential regimes such as Romania. One is the power of the French president to dissolve the parliament. The French president has a powerful legal weapon in the endeavour to increase her convergence with the parliamentary majority, which is not the case in Romania, for example, where majorities are shifting inside one electoral cycle. Second, the French cohabitation usually implies that the prime-minister is strongly attached to (if not directly coming from) the parliamentary majority. Romania is a good case to explore more complex situations including those where the prime minister is endorsed by the president, while the parliamentary majority is hostile to the latter, or where a prime minister initially aligned with the president becomes estranged and builds at some point in the electoral cycle an anti-presidential parliamentary majority.

Moreover, the concept of "cohabitation" focuses on two poles of power, the president and the prime minister, while the parliamentary majority is pushed into the background and fully aligned with the prime minister. My approach is different and sheds light on the "confrontation" between the president and the parliamentary majority. In this analytical framework the prime minister derives her power and authority either from the president or from the governing coalition and the parliamentary majority. With few exceptions, the prime minister is seen only an agent for one of these principals, which vie for the power to influence her. Besides, a dynamic situation with one prime minister that seeks emancipation from a president that used to be a partner cannot be grasped with the static concept of "cohabitation".

Romanian semi-presidentialism

According to the Romanian Constitution, the popularly elected president has the exclusive right to nominate the PM – after formal consultations with the parliamentary parties. Once selected by the president, the PM candidate has ten days to request the confidence of the parliament on the ministerial line-up and the governing programme. The president does not have the formal power to remove ("revoke" – article 7 of the Constitution) the PM. The term of the PM may terminate at the end of the legislative term, following a successful motion of non-confidence or when she decides to step down.

The constitutional provision on the dissolution of the parliament (article 89 of the Constitution) makes the calling of early legislative elections virtually impossible. The president has the formal prerogative to dissolve parliament, but she cannot act in this direction unless two attempts to form a new government have been rejected by the parliament within the time span of 60 days. These requirements have never been met in post-communist Romania. With the exception of the Constitutional Assembly that lasted for two-and-a-half years (May 1990-November 1992), all legislatures since 1992 completed a full four-year term. This had important consequences for the way parliamentary parties handled major political crises – oftentimes triggered by one party of the governing coalition moving to the opposition benches. As crises of this type cannot be resolved through early elections in Romania, party leaders are forced to negotiate new parliamentary majorities during the same electoral cycle (see Ştefan 2004, 2019; Ştefan and Grecu 2014). Presidents and PMs have to act and react in this dynamic environment.

There is another legal provision that has affected the formation of party governments in Romania. According to the law on the organisation and the functioning of the cabinet (Law 90/2001), convicted politicians are barred from being members of the cabinet. This provision prevented Liviu Dragnea, the influential leader of the Social Democratic Party, who was convicted with a suspended sentence, to become PM after the 2016 legislative elections. These circumstances triggered a high level of cabinet instability and many changes at the helm of the government (see below).

The first legislative and presidential elections after democratic transition took place simultaneously in 1990. This continued every four years between 1992 and 2004. A constitutional amendment adopted in 2003 extended the presidential term from four to five years, which paved the way for non-concurrent legislative and presidential terms: parliamentary elections were held every four years (2008, 2012, 2016, 2020), while presidential elections every five years (2009, 2014, 2019). Consequently, the likelihood of a political "cohabitation" between PMs and presidents has significantly increased since 2008 (Table 1).

Table 1 provides a comprehensive view of all the Romanian cabinets, since the first cabinet appointed in the aftermath of the Romanian revolution (Roman I) to the cabinet sworn in in November 2019 (Orban). Both legislative and presidential elections in Romania have been highly competitive. All four presidents had powerful parties or party coalitions behind them, and many PMs have been party chairs or had significant

Table 1. Presidents, prime ministers and party governments in Romania (1989–2019).

Cabinet	Date in	Date out	Way of termination	PM duration[a]	Cabinet duration[a]	Party composition[b]	Cabinet type[c]	PM party credentials[d]	President (party affiliation)	President-parl. majority degree of convergence[e]
Roman I	1989-12-26	1990-05-20	elections	600	145			n.a.	Iliescu (n.a)	
Roman II	1990-06-28	1991-09-26	resignation		455	**FSN**	Mwc	1	Iliescu (FSN)	1
Stolojan	1991-10-17	1992-09-27	elections	346	346	**FSN,** PNL, MER, PDAR	Sur	n.a.	Iliescu (FSN)	1
Vacaroiu I	1992-11-20	1994-08-18	reshuffle	1444	636	**PSD**	Min	n.a.	Iliescu (PSD)	2
Vacaroiu II	1994-08-18	1996-09-03	reshuffle		747	**PSD**, PUNR, (PRM, PSM)	Min	n.a.	Iliescu (PSD)	2
Vacaroiu III	1996-09-03	1996-11-03	elections		61	**PSD**	Min	n.a.	Iliescu (PSD)	2
Ciorbea I	1996-12-12	1997-12-05	reshuffle	464	358	**PNTCD**, PNL, PDL, UDMR, PSDR, PNLCD	Sur	2	Constantinescu (CDR/PNTCD)	2
Ciorbea II	1997-12-05	1998-02-02	reshuffle		59	**PNTCD**, PNL, PDL, UDMR, PSDR	Sur	2	Constantinescu (CDR/PNTCD)	2
Ciorbea III	1998-02-11	1998-03-30	resignation		47	**PNTCD**, PNL, UDMR, PSDR, UFD, (PDL)	Min	2	Constantinescu (CDR/PNTCD)	2
Vasile I	1998-04-17	1998-10-27	reshuffle	605	193	**PNTCD**, PNL, PDL, UDMR, PSDR, UFD	Sur	2	Constantinescu (CDR/PNTCD)	2
Vasile II	1998-10-27	1999-12-13	resignation		412	**PNTCD**, PNL, PDL, UDMR, PSDR	Sur	2	Constantinescu (CDR/PNTCD)	2
Isarescu I	1999-12-22	2000-09-14	reshuffle	340	267	**PNTCD**, PNL, PDL, UDMR, PSDR	Mwc	n.a.	Constantinescu (CDR/PNTCD)	2
Isarescu II	2000-09-14	2000-11-26	elections		73	**PNTCD**, PNL, PDL, UDMR	Min	n.a.	Constantinescu (CDR/PNTCD)	2
Nastase I	2000-12-28	2003-06-19	reshuffle	1431	903	**PSD**, PSDR, PC, (UDMR)	Min	1	Iliescu (PSD)	1
Nastase II	2003-06-19	2004-11-28	elections		528	**PSD**, (UDMR)	Min	1	Iliescu (PSD)	1
Popescu-Tariceanu I	2004-12-29	2006-12-04	reshuffle	1432	705	**PNL**, PDL, UDMR, PC	Min	1	Basescu (PNL-PDL/PDL)	2
Popescu-Tariceanu II	2006-12-04	2007-04-05	reshuffle		122	**PNL**, PDL, UDMR	Min	1	Basescu (PNL-PDL/PDL)	2
Popescu-Tariceanu III	2007-04-05	2008-11-30	elections		605	**PNL**, UDMR, (PSD)	Min	1	Basescu (PDL)	3

Boc I	2008-12-22	2009-10-01	reshuffle	1070	283	**PDL**, PSD	Mwc	1	Basescu (PDL)	2
Boc II	2009-10-01	2009-10-13	censure motion		12	**PDL**	Min	1	Basescu (PDL)	3
Boc III	2009-12-23	2012-02-06	resignation		775	**PDL**, UDMR, UNPR	Min	1	Basescu (PDL)	1
Ungureanu	2012-02-09	2012-04-27	censure motion	78	78	**PDL**, UDMR, UNPR	Min	n.a.	Basescu (PDL)	1
Ponta I	2012-05-07	2012-12-09	elections	1257	216	**PSD**, PNL, PC	Min	1	Basescu (PDL)	3
Ponta II	2012-12-21	2014-02-26	reshuffle		432	**PSD**, PNL, PC, UNPR	Sur	1	Basescu (PDL)	3
Ponta III	2014-03-05	2014-12-17	reshuffle		287	**PSD**, PC, UNPR, UDMR	Min	1	Basescu (PDL)	3
Ponta IV	2014-12-17	2015-11-04	resignation		322	**PSD**, PC, UNPR, PLR	Min	1	Iohannis (PNL)	3
Ciolos	2015-11-17	2016-12-12	elections	391	391	none		n.a.	Iohannis (PNL)	3
Grindeanu	2017-01-04	2017-06-21	censure motion	168	168	**PSD**, ALDE	Mwc	2	Iohannis (PNL)	3
Tudose	2017-06-29	2018-01-15	resignation	200	200	**PSD**, ALDE	Mwc	2	Iohannis (PNL)	3
Dăncilă I	2018-01-29	2019-08-30	reshuffle	644	578	**PSD**, ALDE	Mwc	2	Iohannis (PNL)	3
Dăncilă II	2019-08-30	2019-11-04	censure motion		66	**PSD**	Min	1	Iohannis (PNL)	2
Orban	2019-12-04	2020-02-05	censure motion	94	94	**PNL,** (USR, PMP, UDMR)	Min	1	Iohannis (PNL)	2

Source: author's compilation.

[a]The horizontal lines demarcate parliamentary terms. Office duration in days.

[b]Party of PM marked in bold; parties ordered by parliamentary size; support parties of minority cabinets indicated in brackets.

[c]MIN – minority; MWC – minimal winning coalition; SUR – surplus coalition.

[d]1 – Top party leadership; 2 – Some party credentials; n.a. – No party credentials (no party affiliation).

[e]1 – Strong convergence, 2 – Weak convergence, 3 – No convergence.

party credentials. Five out of the 16 PMs, however, had no party affiliation when they were nominated. Office duration of PMs varies greatly, even under one and the same president. Most PMs ran multiple cabinets, supported by parliamentary majorities with different composition. And the other way around: the same parliamentary majority (and the same president) saw PMs coming and going (Vasile/Isarescu, Boc/Ungureanu, Grindeanu/Tudose/Dancila). This variation will be explained when considering each president in relationship with each of PMs who served under her on the background of the convergence or lack thereof between the president and the parliamentary majority.

Prime ministers and presidents in post-communist Romania: empirical analysis

In accordance with the focus on the presidential power over PMs in Romania, the following analysis is structured along the terms of the four presidents. The description of the political processes and the assessments over the relative power of presidents, PMs and parliamentary majorities is based on the close observation of Romanian politics of this author who has been studying and writing on this subject for more than 20 years. Insights into the nuts and bolts of Romanian politics have been acquired during the research investigations whose main findings have been published in Stefan (2004, 2019) and Ştefan and Grecu (2014) among others. Data comes from various books and journal articles published in Romanian and English (e.g. Abraham 2016; King and Sum 2011; Pavel and Huiu 2003; Ştefănescu 2011; Voiculescu 2014).

Ion Iliescu (1990–1996, 2000–2004)

Ion Iliescu was elected to the presidential office three times (1990, 1992 and 2000). He chaired the National Salvation Front (FSN), which came to power after the collapse of communism in December 1989 and chose *Petre Roman* as the first post-communist PM. Iliescu won the first presidential elections in the first round, with 86 percent of the votes. After FSN won the first parliamentary elections in June 1990 with 66 percent of the vote and set up a majority government of its own, Roman remained in PM office and took over the FSN leadership from Iliescu. However, the latter remained in full control of the party and the parliamentary majority (*strong convergence*). The president's predominant position over the PM manifested itself one year later when deep conflicts between the two regarding economic and political reforms emerged. Although Roman had consolidated his public image as a reformist PM and started to assert his authority over FSN, the president forced him out from office in a context of social unrest triggered by unpopular measures taken by the government.

Thereafter, Iliescu picked a "politically emasculated" candidate for PM: *Theodor Stolojan,* a technocrat with no party credentials who posed no threat to him. Even though FSN split in two (one party led by Roman, later becoming the Liberal-Democratic Party – PDL, and another one led informally by Iliescu, the Social-Democratic Party – PSD), Iliescu at no point lost the control over the parliamentary majority and was able to keep his preferred PM in office.

After the 1992 elections, the PSD commanded only 34% of the parliamentary seats. To get the investiture vote, it relied on three left-leaning nationalistic parties (PUNR, PRM,

PSM). However, these parties were not willing to provide full and unconditional support for the entire legislative term (*weak convergence*). As newly reelected president, Iliescu easily imposed the technocrat *Nicolae Vacaroiu* as PM, but had difficulties in keeping him in office. Vacaroiu survived a motion of non-confidence filed in 1993, but the threat of a new one pushed both the president and the PM to solidify the cabinet's parliamentary support. Eventually, agreements with the three above mentioned parties were signed in 1995 leading to a PSD-PUNR coalition government. PRM and PSM did not take cabinet seats, but committed to provide parliamentary support to the new cabinet. Therefore, the president had to give in to other parliamentary parties in order to keep his favourite PM in place.

Iliescu lost the 1996 presidential elections, but returned as president in 2000. At the 2000 legislative elections, PSD's victory was clearer than in 1992 (45% of parliamentary seats). The resulting governing coalition between PSD and PC which was supported by the party of Hungarian minority (UDMR) turned out to be stable and solid (*strong convergence*). Like Roman in 1990, *Adrian Nastase* took over the PM office and the party leadership following Iliescu's move to the presidential palace. Although Nastase was a powerful PM, with tight control over the party and the cabinet, he was loyal and ideologically closer to Iliescu than Roman.

Emil Constantinescu (1996–2000)

In 1996, the Romanian Democratic Convention (CDR), an umbrella of various political parties and civic associations, won both the legislative and the presidential elections. Emil Constantinescu, the chair of CDR, became elected president. The Christian-Democratic National Peasants' Party (PNTCD) was the leading force of the CDR, while the National Liberal Party (PNL) was only the second fiddle. Constantinescu was formally a PNTCD member, but never held a senior position in the party. After the elections, CDR formed a governing coalition with PDL and UDMR. Although on the same page with Constantinescu when it came to major reform policies, the parliamentary majority was heterogeneous – which made compromises with the president difficult to reach (*weak convergence*).

Upon his election and at the peak of his popularity, Constantinescu selected *Victor Ciorbea* as PM. Ciorbea was a trade union leader who joined the CDR earlier in 1996, had only loose affiliation to the PNTCD, but boasted an impressive victory in Bucharest mayoral elections six months before. Soon after taking office, conflicts between the PM and the major government parties began to multiply. Ciorbea was still in control when the cabinet was reshuffled in December 1997. Ciorbea's second cabinet, however, stumbled on an ultimatum by PDL, whose leaders threatened the president that unless Ciorbea steps down, PDL ministers would resign and jeopardise the stability of the governing coalition. Initially the president resisted the pressures from the PDL, and the latter left the cabinet in February 1998. However, intra-governmental demands to remove the PM did not subside. On the contrary, PNL and even Constantinescu's own PNTCD asked for Ciorbea's resignation. Reluctantly, the president convinced the PM to resign in March 1998.

In order to calm down the tensions with the government parties, Constantinescu asked the PNTCD General Secretary *Radu Vasile* to form a cabinet. By choosing a PM with more party credentials, Constantinescu hoped that the new PM would not be discharged so easily by the leaders of the coalition parties. However, after accession to PM office, Vasile distanced himself from his own party (PNTCD) and found support inside PDL and PNL. Unlike Ciorbea, he also started to confront Constantinescu within a year after assuming the PM office. This time, it was the president who tried to remove the PM, but Vasile resisted as much as he could. Constantinescu issued a decree to revoke the PM, although this measure was unconstitutional and with no immediate effect. It was not until PNTCD withdrew its political support and PNL turned the back on him that Vasile stepped down.

Like Iliescu after getting rid of turbulent Roman, Constantinescu selected his third PM from outside the political parties. He entrusted *Mugur Isarescu*, then the Governor of Romania's National Bank, with the formation of a new government in December 1999. The same parties shared the ministerial portfolios and continued to provide parliamentary support to the cabinet. With three rounds of elections in 2000 (local, legislative and presidential), the government parties focused more on preparing the campaigns than on agreeing on major policies. Isarescu and his cabinet were very much left alone and perceived much more like having a caretaking mission. One small left-wing party left the governing coalition (leading to the second Isarescu cabinet) to enter into a pre-electoral agreement with PSD, the main opposition party.

Traian Basescu (2004–2014)

Basescu was the first Romanian president to benefit from the extension of the presidential mandate from four to five years and the first one witnessing non-concurrent parliamentary and presidential elections during his two terms. In 2004, however, presidential and parliamentary elections took place – for the last time before 2024 – at the same time. The victory was split: Basescu, the candidate of the PNL-PDL coalition, won the presidential elections, while PSD together with its longstanding partner PC won the legislative elections. Capitalising on his strong popular mandate, Basescu negotiated with UDMR and PC and convinced them to form a parliamentary majority together with PNL and PDL. The outcome of these successful negotiations was a coalition cabinet of four parties led by the PNL chair, *Calin Popescu-Tariceanu*. Basescu used to share the leadership of the PNL-PDL coalition with Tariceanu and had a limited grasp on the other two junior parties of the governing coalition, resulting in *weak political convergence* between him and the parliamentary majority. Centrifugal tendencies between the governing parties became visible since 2005 and eventually led the PC to exit the coalition and join the PSD in the opposition.

Such tensions also emerged between PNL and PDL as well as between the president and the PM. In May 2005, Tariceanu refused to endorse Basescu's plan to call for early elections. The president turned all his energies against the PM hoping to remove him. However, not only did Tariceanu withstand the pressure, but also managed to form an anti-presidential coalition in parliament. In April 2007, PNL turned to opposition PSD for support, in exchange for backing PSD's attempt to impeach the president. An informal coalition between PNL and PSD (joined by UDMR, PC and other opposition parties) provided parliamentary support to a minority PNL-UDMR cabinet (Tariceanu III). As a result of *no convergence* between president and the parliament, Tariceanu survived as PM until the end of the legislative term, while PDL and President Basescu were isolated. This conflictual constellation led to the first attempt to impeach the president in April 2007. Basescu was suspended for a month by parliament, but returned to his office following a referendum in which a popular majority voted in his favour.

At the 2008 legislative elections, PSD won the majority of popular votes while PDL won a majority of seats in parliament – an oddity of a mixed electoral system. Against the background of the economic crisis, Basescu used his formal and informal powers to forge an uneasy "grand" coalition between PSD and PDL. His main condition was that PDL chair Emil Boc, Basescu's closest aid since 2004, becomes PM. The president remained influential inside the PDL, but PSD was still driven by a strong feeling against him. The *weak and fragile convergence* between Basescu and the PDL-PSD parliamentary majority was brought to an end in the run-up to 2009 presidential elections, as PSD moved to the opposition, leaving Boc with a rump cabinet (Boc II). In the situation of *no convergence*, Basescu's favourite PM Boc was removed following the first-ever successful motion of non-confidence in post-communist Romania.

In the aftermath of his reelection in December 2009, Basescu was again able to shape a pro-presidential majority around PDL – with UDMR and a splinter group from PSD called UNPR (*strong convergence*). *Emil Boc*, a former PM loyal to Basescu, was again called to run the government. This was the beginning of a relatively long period of political stability. The third Boc cabinet stayed in office for more than two years, a real achievement given the volatility of Romanian politics in general. However, this was also the period when painful austerity measures have been adopted, which led to increased public hostility towards the president, the PM and the PDL-led cabinet. In order to save face, and redress the standing in the polls of the PDL, Basescu replaced Boc with a technocrat *Mihai Razvan Ungureanu*, the head of the foreign intelligence service, with no formal partisan affiliation.

Ungureanu was supported by the same parties that supported the last Boc cabinet, but soon he managed to antagonise not only junior parties of the coalition, but even the major governing party (PDL). UNPR and allegedly some PDL legislators supported a motion of non-confidence against the Ungureanu cabinet initiated by PSD, PNL and PC – now reunited in a formal political alliance called Social-Liberal Union (USL). For the third time in almost eight years, Basescu had to cope with a hostile parliamentary majority (*no convergence*). Like five years before, the new parliamentary majority formed around PSD and PNL decided to impeach the president once again.

Basescu survived this second impeachment, but the *lack of convergence* with parliamentary majority considerably narrowed his political room for maneuver. In May 2012, he had to accept *Victor Ponta*, the leader of the main opposition party (PSD), as PM. After the 2012 legislative elections and the crushing victory of the PSD-PNL alliance (60% vs. 16% for PDL), president Basescu was left with no other option than to endorse Ponta as the head of a PSD-PNL cabinet for the second time. There were no big changes until February 2014, when PNL left the Ponta II cabinet and re-established the alliance with PDL. However, PM Ponta was able to keep the control of the parliamentary majority who voted for his reshuffled cabinet after UDMR has decided to become the junior governing partner (Ponta III). The *lack of convergence* between president Basescu and the parliamentary majority lasted until the end of his second term in December 2014. Basescu was at odds with Ponta in all these years, but had no leverage to block his projects or remove him from office.

Klaus Iohannis (2014–2019)

The re-establishment of the PDL-PNL partnership in February 2014 led to two major developments. On the one hand, the two parties merged and decided to nominate Klaus Iohannis, the popular mayor of Sibiu, as their presidential candidate. Iohannis had joined the PNL one year before, but took over its chairmanship only in the run-up to the presidential elections. On the other hand, a party called ALDE splintered from PNL, became PSD's main political partner and provided parliamentary support to Ponta's government.

Iohannis defeated the PSD candidate, the then incumbent PM *Ponta*, at the presidential elections, but his victory had limited impact on the parliamentary majority. Ponta preserved his prime-ministerial position as he managed to find sufficient parliamentary support even after his defeat: UDMR left the cabinet, but was replaced by ALDE (*no convergence*).

When the anti-corruption directorate opened an investigation against the PM six months into his first term, Iohannis asked publicly for Ponta's resignation. Ponta was backed by the parliament and felt immune to president's repeated calls for resignation. However, a fire in a nightclub with dozens of casualties triggered a social uproar which led to resignation of PM Ponta. The public opinion turned not only against Ponta, his party and his cabinet but also against all mainstream parties that were accused of corruption and neglect of public interests. Against this background, in November 2015 Iohannis successfully pushed for a technocratic government led by non-affiliated *Dacian Ciolos*, a former member of the European Commission. Parties forming the parliamentary majority accepted this unusual solution, although there was *no political convergence* with the president. The PM could remain in office until the end of the term only because parliamentary parties were already preparing for the 2016 legislative elections. Being the dominant party in the parliament, PSD chose to stay in opposition in order to build a better case against Iohannis and the government.

This strategy paid off as PSD won 47 percent of the seats following the 2016 legislative elections. PSD and ALDE formed a coalition, while UDMR agreed to support the cabinet from the parliament. PNL, the party of the president, controlled only 21 percent of the seats and did not have the resources to forge a pro-presidential parliamentary majority.

Until mid-2019, Iohannis faced a hostile parliament (*no convergence*). It was therefore difficult for him to reject the prime-ministerial proposals put forward by PSD: *Sorin Grindeanu*, *Mihai Tudose*, and *Viorica Dancila*. As indicated before, Liviu Dragnea (the PSD chair) was barred from assuming PM position due to a suspended prison sentence. In order to implement his will and vision, he needed a loyal proxy. President Iohannis did neither influence the nomination of the three PSD PMs nor the deselection of Grindeanu and Tudose, which were ousted by the PSD as they stepped out of the lines imposed by Liviu Dragnea. Viorica Dancila had a completely different fate, since she acted subservient to Dragnea and followed closely his political instructions. She held the PM position when Dragnea was imprisoned following another corruption-related sentence. Dancila not only took over the party leadership from Dragnea, but also became PSD's presidential candidate. President Iohannis asked publicly for her resignation, as he did with Ponta four years ago, especially for the way she handled foreign affairs. But the president's public pressures had no effect. What triggered her dismissal and the change in the government was the break of the PSD-ALDE coalition and ALDE's decision to support a motion of non-confidence filed by PNL. All parliamentary parties except for PSD agreed to hand over the government to PNL, thus forming a heterogeneous parliamentary majority aligned with the president (*weak convergence*). Under these circumstances, Iohannis managed to impose *Ludovic Orban*, the chair of PNL, as PM. Within three months, the fragile government majority collapsed as PSD managed to muster enough parliamentary support to take down the Orban cabinet in February 2020.

Conclusion

Empirical evidence from Romania confirms the major hypothesis of this article. In relationship to PMs, presidents can predominate, yield to PM or evolve from one constellation to another. Given the long tenures of Romanian presidents and the shorter durations of cabinets and parliamentary majorities, variation was observable during the entire term(s) of each president. This variation is explained through the political convergence of the president with the parliamentary majority.

Although Romanian presidents do not have constitutional powers to dismiss PMs, they can nevertheless initiate and steer the process through which a PM eventually leaves office. This is a direct consequence of their popular legitimacy, but also of their undisputed influence in the parties they used to lead before taking up the presidential office. In most of the cases of strong or weak convergence presented in this article, presidents remained supportive of their PMs for their entire tenure. Three PMs turned the back to the president, with only one (Calin Popescu Tariceanu) surviving the wrath of the head of state. The other two (Petre Roman in 1991 and Radu Vasile in 1999) had to step down before the end of the term following presidential calls for resignation. In case of strong convergence, the president could dispose of the PM, even if he was non-conflictual and chaired the governing party (the case of Emil Boc in 2012).

PM survival in circumstances of weak convergence also depended on factors that the president could not entirely control. Nicolae Vacaroiu was one of the longest serving PMs, but he needed the skills and the full support of the president to resist in office for a full four-year term given a very unstable parliamentary basis. Victor Ciorbea came under heavy attack from one party of the governing coalition and had to step down. Calin Popescu-Tariceanu turned from a friend to a foe of the president and was able to create an anti-presidential parliamentary majority. Emil Boc in 2009, Mihai Razvan Ungureanu in 2012 and Ludovic Orban in 2020 fell victims to similar changes in the political direction and composition of the parliamentary majority. In these three cases, the presidential endorsement was not of much help – on the contrary.

The powers of the president are severely limited in cases of no convergence with the parliamentary majority. They have little influence on the nomination of the PMs and have practically no means of removing them from office. As the analysis shows, president Basescu could not do much against PM Popescu-Tariceanu after the latter found unexpected support in the major opposition party. Similarly, he could neither oppose the nomination of Victor Ponta as PM nor oust him from office. President Iohannis had to work with incumbent PM Ponta and also accept the three ensuing PM nominations made by PSD.

In sum, PMs are not necessarily puppets in the hands of the president. Indeed, the president may be the sole responsible for their nomination in convergent constellations, but prime-ministerial survival is a different issue. Depending on the circumstances (weak or strong convergence), the PMs have to be careful to other political players, opposition parties, but also to parties from the governing coalition. PMs may rebel and take their fate in their own hands and – if skilful – may survive even against the president's wish (Tariceanu's endurance is a good example in this regard). The key is to build an anti-presidential majority in parliament. This is even more the case in cases of no convergence: PMs are real players, contending for political supremacy with the president.

Further explorations of this topic should take even more into consideration the dynamic character of the interactions between president, parliamentary majorities and PMs. Parliamentary majorities may change during the course of a legislative term, sometimes as a result of president or PM's interference. Powerful presidents may be significantly weakened by coalitions between "rebel" PMs and parliamentary majorities. Last but not least, PMs strongly backed by the president are forced to terminate their tenure if disliked by the (new) parliamentary majorities. In pluralist societies with enduring political and social cleavages, with a balanced party system and a functional system of checks and balances, these power games are part of a vibrant democratic system. But only a systematic analysis of these complex interactions allows us to take the understanding of democratic processes to a superior level, beyond the simple description of the winners and losers of legislative and presidential elections.

Disclosure statement

No potential conflict of interest was reported by the author(s).

ORCID

Laurenţiu Ştefan (i) http://orcid.org/0000-0002-3725-9425

References

Abraham, Florin. 2016. *Romania Since the Second World War. A Political, Social and Economic History.* London: Bloomsbury Academic.

Baylis, Thomas A. 2007. "Embattled Executives: Prime Ministerial Weakness in East Central Europe." *Communist and Post-Communist Studies* 40 (1): 81–106.

Blondel, Jean, and Ferdinand Müller-Rommel, eds. 2001. *Cabinets in Eastern Europe.* London: Palgrave.

Elgie, Robert. 2010. "Semi-Presidentialism, Cohabitation and the Collapse of Electoral Democracies, 1990–2008." *Government and Opposition* 45 (1): 29–49.

Grotz, Florian, and Till Weber. 2017. "Prime Ministerial Tenure in Central and Eastern Europe: The Role of Party Leadership and Cabinet Experience." In *Parties, Governments and Elites: The Comparative Study of Democracy*, edited by Philipp Harfst, Ina Kubbe, and Thomas Poguntke, 225–244. Wiesbaden: Springer.

King, Ronald F., and Paul E. Sum, eds. 2011. *Romania Under Băsescu: Aspirations, Achievements, and Frustrations During His First Presidential Term.* Lanham: Lexington Books.

Marrani, David. 2009. "Semi-presidentialism à la française: the Recent Consitutional Evolution of the Two-headed Executive." *Constitutional Forum* 18 (2): 69–77.

Pavel, Dan, and Iulia Huiu. 2003. *Nu putem reuşi decât împreună. O istorie analitică a Convenţiei Democratice 1989–2000* [Toghether, We Can Succeed: An Analytical History of the Democratic Convention 1989–2000]. Iaşi: Editura Polirom.

Protsyk, Oleh. 2005. "Politics of Intraexecutive Conflict in Semipresidential Regimes in Eastern Europe." *East European Politics and Societies: and Cultures* 19 (2): 135–160.

Samuels, David J., and Matthew S. Shugart. 2010. *Presidents, Parties and Prime Ministers: How the Separation of Powers Affects Party Organization and Behavior.* Cambridge: Cambridge University Press.

Sedelius, Thomas, and Joakim Ekman. 2010. "Intra-Executive Conflict and Cabinet Instability: Effects of Semi-Presidentialism in Central and Eastern Europe." *Government and Opposition* 45 (4): 505–530.

Ştefan, Laurenţiu. 2004. *Patterns of Political Elite Recruitment in Post-Communist Romania.* Bucharest: Ziua Publishing House.

Ştefan, Laurenţiu. 2019. "Romania: Presidential Politics and Coalition Bargaining." In *Coalition Governments in East and Central Europe*, edited by Wolfgang C. Müller, Torbjörn Bergman, and Gabriella Ilonszki, 388–434. Oxford: Oxford University Press.

Ştefan, Laurenţiu, and Răzvan Grecu. 2014. "The 'Waiting Room': Romanian Parliament after 1989." In *Parliamentary Elites in Central and Eastern Europe: Recruitment and Representation*, edited by Elena Semenova, Michael Edinger, and Heinrich Best, 194–215. London: Routledge.

Ştefănescu, Domniţa. 2011. *11 ani din istoria României, decembrie 1989–decembrie 2000. O cronologie a evenimentelor* [Romanian History: December 1989-December 2000 – A Chronology]. Bucharest: Editura Maşina de scris.

Voiculescu, Dan. 2014. *Uniunea Social Liberală. Ideea care l-a îngenuncheat pe Băsescu Traian* [The Social-Liberal Union: The Idea that Put Down Basescu Traian]. Bucharest: Editura Rao.

CONCLUSION

Weak chief executives? Post-communist prime ministers between their parties, parliaments and presidents

Marko Kukec ⓘ and Florian Grotz ⓘ

This chapter concludes this volume on Prime Ministers (PMs) and party governments in Central and Eastern Europe (CEE). It provides a synthesis of the findings on the major factors which stabilize PMs in three arenas: their own party, other parliamentary parties and the dual executive. With a tight control of their parties, party-leader PMs stay longer in office even in circumstances which threaten to mobilize intra-party resistance. While majority cabinets provide an obvious advantage when dealing with other parliamentary parties, some PMs heading minority cabinets successfully employed other instruments to remain in office. The attempts of state presidents to assume control over executive are best countered by PMs who secured the support of their own party and the parliamentary majority.

The survival of prime ministers in the post-communist context

The institutional position of PMs in CEE did not emerge from a careful constitutional design, leaving the prime-ministerial office somewhat neglected and exposed to pressures from other political actors (Malová and Haughton 2002, 107). The general weakness of PMs in CEE, indicated by their relatively short office duration, has raised concerns about the overall stability and functioning of post-communist democracies (Baylis 2007). Nevertheless, several case studies point out PMs in different CEE countries and time periods who resisted such pressures and remained in office long enough to leave a substantive political legacy (Buchowski 2020; Cirhan and Kopecký 2020). This volume seeks to account for this apparent variation, by systematically exploring the survival of PMs as dependent on the conditions within three political arenas: the PM's own party, other parliamentary parties and the dual executive shared with state presidents. The theoretical framework identifies several individual and contextual factors that assist PMs to prevail in their interrelation with other political actors within the three arenas.

Beyond the institutional and political context, PMs in CEE operate under difficult economic circumstances. As a consequence of the transition to market economy and recurrent crises (e.g., the Russian financial crisis in 1998 and the global financial crisis in 2008), many PMs in the region had to cope with substantial budget deficits, unemployment rates, inflation and sluggish economic growth (Backlund, Ecker, and Meyer 2019). These unfavorable economic conditions placed an additional strain on the interrelations between PMs and other political actors, as they limited the ability of governments to finance social programs or invest into critical infrastructure. However, the effects of economic hardship on prime-ministerial survival seem to be ambiguous. While some PMs resigned or were removed from office due to their failure to address unemployment and budget deficits, others have used the context of economic difficulties to showcase their crisis management skills and secure their position vis-à-vis other political actors.

Against this background, the preceding contributions have explored prime-ministerial duration in a systematic comparative overview in the eleven countries of CEE and in relevant case studies. Following the presentation of empirical material, this chapter provides a synthesis of the volume's findings. Proceeding along the framework elaborated in the introductory chapter, we first review the interaction between PMs and their parties, followed by their success in securing support of other parliamentary parties, and their relations within the dual executive. The final section restates the major power resources of PMs and advances their relevance for prime-ministerial performance in office.

Prime ministers and their parties

The interrelationship between the PM and her own party is a delicate balance. On the one hand, prime-ministerial parties have developed mechanisms to monitor and sanction their heads of government who depart from their policy agenda or get involved in a political scandal. The mechanism of last resort is the replacement of the PM within the parliamentary term, either through a formal intra-party vote or through informal pressure. On the other hand, the prime-ministerial party is the key political ally of the PM, with a keen interest in the success of its appointee to the most powerful political office in a parliamentary democracy.

In the introductory chapter, we argued that party leadership of PM is the decisive condition to maintain the constant support of her party even in difficult circumstances. Party leaders come to office following a rigorous selection process, during which the candidate establishes a support base within the party and emerges as the most visible party member in public. The general patterns of prime-ministerial selection and survival in CEE between 1990 and 2019 confirm the importance of party leadership for PMs. In most countries, the considerable majority of PMs were either party leaders before assuming the prime-ministerial office or became party leaders shortly thereafter. Moreover, party-leader PMs have survived longer in office (950 days on average) than those who were not party leaders (459 days on average).

Two contributions to this book reflect on the concrete mechanisms on how party leadership affected the possibilities of PMs to maintain the support of their own parties and ultimately to survive in office. More specifically, Alenka Krašovec and Dario Nikić-Čakar explore the conditions under which Croatian and Slovenian PMs secure their survival when genuinely new parties (GNPs) are included in coalition governments. For this purpose, they select the Croatian PMs Tihomir Orešković and Andrej Plenković as well as the Slovenian PMs Alenka Bratušek and Miro Cerar. The two former PMs led cabinets with a GNP as a junior coalition partner, whereas the latter ones themselves originated from a GNP. Similarly, the contribution of Maria Spirova and Radostina Sharenkova-Toshkova considers the case of Bulgarian PM Boyko Borissov who founded his own party.

Orešković and Bratušek assumed prime-ministerial office after the leaders of their respective parties (Karamarko of HDZ and Janković of PS) withdrew their candidacy for strategic reasons. Nevertheless, the party leaders exerted continuous pressure on these PMs, which was reinforced by the participation of new parties in coalition cabinets. The cabinet of the technocrat Orešković included the GNP Most, which kept its anti-establishment attitude even after entering government, by criticizing the major policy initiatives coming from the senior coalition party HDZ. Orešković attempted to act as a mediator between the two coalition partners, at one point even demanding their leaders to resign as deputy PMs. Karamarko responded by filing a no-confidence motion against the government, and with PM Orešković lacking any support within HDZ, the motion was adopted by the parliamentary majority. PM Bratušek was similarly involved in a personal conflict with Janković, who sought to influence the governmental policies using his powerful role as the founder and de-facto leader of PS. Their power struggle culminated during the party leadership contest in 2014, in which Janković prevailed, followed by the resignation of Bratušek as PM.

By contrast, Borissov, Cerar and Plenković were the leaders of their parties, which made their survival in prime-ministerial office much easier. The first two were founders and leaders of GNPs (SMC and GERB), allowing them to secure the support of their parties even when the difficult reality of government participation became obvious for them. For instance, Borissov extensively used the personnel policy, by gradually replacing outsider ministers with a core group of GERB party activists. Compared to his technocratic predecessor, PM Plenković was able to secure strong support within the HDZ. This gave him freedom to exchange the new party Most as a coalition partner for the established party HNS, which came from the opposite leftist bloc of the Croatian party system and was more reliable.

Prime ministers and other parliamentary parties

Beyond the support of their own parties, PMs are dependent on other parliamentary parties to survive in office. Hence, the breakup of a governing coalition often provokes the end of prime-ministerial tenure. The overall patterns which we presented in the introductory chapter seem to confirm this assumption. More specifically, the average durations of PMs and party governments in CEE democracies differ only in about 70 days. However, the results for individual countries uncover different dynamics in the relationship between PMs and party governments. Most remarkably, some PMs have been successful in reorganizing the partisan composition of their cabinets and survived in office, a pattern most clearly observed in Croatia and Slovenia. In fewer cases, the partisan composition of the government coalition endured, while PM was exchanged.

From the plethora of conditions which affect the stability of PMs and party governments, we selected two which are particularly relevant in the post-communist context. First, minority governments have been a frequent phenomenon in several CEE countries (Keudel-Kaiser 2016). They are problematic for the PMs, as they usually entail the lack of credible commitment by the supporting parties in parliament and may bring down the government at any point. Our comparative analysis of cabinet duration finds that minority cabinets in CEE are indeed at the higher risk of early termination than majority cabinets. Second, the government participation of GNPs is considered to have a detrimental impact on cabinet governance and survival. Due to their recent origin, GNPs have less experienced personnel in parliament and the executive and attempt to more clearly distinguish themselves from their established coalition partners. However, despite these characteristics, their cabinet participation does not generally increase the risk of early cabinet termination compared to cabinets with established parties only. The important condition is whether GNP nominates the PM or acts as a junior partner to an established party.

The mechanisms behind the effect of minority status and involvement of GNPs on prime-ministerial survival are explored by three contributions to this volume. The Hungarian case study demonstrates that the repercussions of minority governments for prime-ministerial strength may be mitigated through ideological moderation. Daniel Kovarek compares the political success of PMs who led the only two minority governments in post-communist Hungary: Ferenc Gyurcsány (2008–2009) and Gordon Bajnai (2009–2010). While the two MSZP minority cabinets were supported by the same party (SZDSZ), Bajnai was considerably more successful in attaining the support of SZDSZ for his legislative agenda than his predecessor. Daniel Kovarek links the relative success of Bajnai to his strategy of ideological moderation. By contrast, Gyurcsány continued to pursue a highly partisan political agenda, which was rejected by the SZDSZ.

Croatia and Slovenia have experienced a recent surge of GNPs in parliaments and governments. As Alenka Krašovec and Dario Nikić-Čakar argue, the government participation of these parties has placed considerable strain on the survival of both PMs and their party governments. An obvious case is the Croatian GNP Most, which failed to formulate a clear policy direction beyond the continuous criticism of proposals coming from its coalition partner HDZ. Similarly, Miro Cerar's party SMC owned its electoral success to the personality of its leader but otherwise lacked a clear policy agenda and experienced personnel. In response to these challenges, Slovenian and Croatian PMs attempted to ensure their survival through various strategies. Their success critically depended on their individual capabilities and power resources, as in the case of Cerar in Slovenia who skillfully combined formal and informal mechanisms of cabinet conflict management or Plenković in Croatia who succeeded to remove the rebellious GNP from his government.

The Bulgarian PM Boyko Borissov (2009–2013; 2014–2017) experienced an exceptionally difficult party constellation, coming from a GNP and heading a minority government during both of his terms. Against the unfavorable odds, he became the longest-serving PM in the country. The contribution by Maria Spirova and Radostina Sharenkova-Toshkova attributes the surprising survival of Borissov to the combination of early organizational consolidation of his party GERB and building of personal following, which pre-empted the shortage of experienced and loyal cadre for executive offices. Beyond these more conventional procedures, the authors single out Borissov's strategic resignations from PM office, by which he successfully deflected the responsibility of his government for poor economic conditions and removed problematic coalition partners at the same time.

Prime ministers and state presidents

Tensions within the dual executives are common in parliamentary democracies, but the directly elected presidents in several CEE countries place PMs into a particularly precarious position. Presidents with a popular mandate and extensive institutional powers have sought to influence governmental policies in various domains and to gain control over the cabinet composition. In several intra-executive conflicts, presidents have used formal and informal instruments to provoke the departure of PMs from their office. On the other hand, presidents have also been important allies of PMs, which stabilized the position of the latter.

The patterns of prime-ministerial duration in CEE reveal considerable variation in presidential powers and their partisan congruence with PMs. Presidents command different levels of legislative and non-legislative competencies, which do not neatly follow the mode of (direct or indirect) presidential elections. Moreover, there is a general balance in the partisan constellations between presidents and PMs, as, in addition to congruence and cohabitation, we observed almost 30% of PM-president dyads where the president was independent. Despite the considerable variation, the constitutional powers of presidents and the occurrence of cohabitation individually have weak and rather inconsistent effects on the ability of PMs to retain their office. The effect becomes somewhat clearer only when these two factors are analyzed in conjunction, as particularly those presidents that are institutionally powerful and opposition-affiliated present the greatest challenge for prime-ministerial survival. The relevant countries where this was observed are Romania, Hungary and Slovakia.

To get a more nuanced understanding of the relationships between PMs and state presidents and their impact on prime-ministerial survival, two contributions to the book have dealt with the cases of Lithuania and Romania. As mentioned in the introduction, both countries are characterized by directly elected and constitutionally powerful state presidents. Against this background, both chapters broadly explore the relevance of partisan congruence for the power of PMs. Laurențiu Ștefan delves deeper into the interactive effect of presidential powers and partisan congruence, which we detected in the comparative overview. Lukas Pukelis and Mažvydas Jastramskis focus on the influence of independent presidents on the PMs' discretion over cabinet composition, which has largely escaped the extant literature on cohabitation in semi-presidential regimes.

The contribution by Laurențiu Ștefan confirms the overall pattern reported in the introductory chapter. When Romanian presidents are influential figures in one of the governing parties, they exert control over PMs through two mechanisms. On the one hand, they may use their authority to facilitate coalition formation and management, thus assisting PMs in securing the support of the parliamentary majority. On the other hand, presidents commanding government parties may force PMs to leave office, despite not having the formal prerogative of cabinet dissolution. However, when the PM is in control of her own party and enjoys the support of the parliamentary majority, Romanian presidents have limited possibilities to assert their dominance within the executive. Lukas Pukelis and Mažvydas Jastramskis show that independent presidents in Lithuania sought active involvement in ministerial selection, and from 30 such instances, they were successful in 24. As in the Romanian case, such presidential activism is constrained when a PM enjoys strong parliamentary support while it increases when presidents receive a fresh electoral mandate.

Summary and outlook

The individual contributions to this volume provide a systematic and differentiated picture of prime-ministerial survival across the eleven CEE democracies. Structured along the three arenas within which PMs need to secure support of key political actors, the contributions identified a core set of conditions which enable PMs to remain in office. In particular, both the quantitative patterns and the case studies confirm that PMs who are party leaders and lead a majority government have the best chances to complete the full prime-ministerial term. In such constellation, PMs are able to resist the challenges of new parties in cabinet, even when they themselves emerge from one, as well as constrain the state president to the role as "dignified part" of the constitution.

Several contributions highlight that PMs do not depend exclusively on a single arena but rather on the constellation of actors in multiple arenas. Indeed, the analysis of individual cases reveals a more complex picture, with important implications for our understanding of prime-ministerial survival in post-communist democracies. Most interestingly, the weakness of PMs in a single arena may be compensated by their strong position within another arena. For example, several Romanian PMs successfully resisted the pressure of opposition-affiliated presidents by relying on the backing of their own party or the support of their parliamentary allies. Another common thread running through most contributions is the importance of individual skills of PMs in maintaining their office. Remarkably, certain PMs survived under exceptionally difficult conditions. A case in point is the Bulgarian PM Borissov, who successfully ensured his survival in office despite leading a minority cabinet predominantly composed of new parties, including his own GERB. This observation implies that studies of PMs and their interactions with the three arenas should more carefully consider their individual predispositions and explore them in conjunction with contextual factors.

The comparative analysis of prime-ministerial survival, as indicated by office duration, complements the studies focusing on the substantive tasks PMs ought to perform during their term. Apart from their survival skills and support of own parties and parliamentary majority which keep them in office, PMs also need to provide direction for domestic policy, manage their cabinets, secure national interests abroad, and cope with exogenous crises (Strangio, 't Hart, and Walter 2013; 't Hart and Schelfhout 2016; Grotz et al. 2021). Reflecting the findings of this volume, post-communist PMs perform these tasks more successfully when having experience as party leaders, which confirms that party leadership is the most important resource for the PMs in the region. At the same time, minority governments do not appear to be a disadvantage for prime-ministerial performance, while their survival is considerably constrained under such constellation (Grotz et al. 2021). Hence, future studies might explore the mutual interdependence of prime-ministerial survival and performance, which allows for a more holistic assessment of the strength of PMs and their impact on democratic governance and stability.

Acknowledgements

We would especially like to thank Ferdinand Müller-Rommel, the anonymous reviewer and the participants of a workshop held at Helmut Schmidt University, Hamburg, on 18–20 September 2019 on which first drafts of the papers included in this Special Issue were discussed.

Disclosure statement

No potential conflict of interest was reported by the authors.

Funding

We gratefully acknowledge the generous funding by the German Research Foundation (DFG) (Grants GR3311/3-1 and MU618/18-1).

ORCID

Marko Kukec http://orcid.org/0000-0002-9453-2977
Florian Grotz http://orcid.org/0000-0002-7512-2526

References

Backlund, Anders, Alejandro Ecker, and Thomas M. Meyer. 2019. "The Economic and Political Context of Coalition Politics in Central Eastern Europe." In *Coalition Governance in Central Eastern Europe*, edited by Torbjörn Bergman, Gabriella Ilonszki, and Wolfgang C. Müller, 60–85. Oxford: Oxford University Press.

Baylis, Thomas A. 2007. "Embattled Executives: Prime Ministerial Weakness in East Central Europe." *Communist and Post-Communist Studies* 40 (1): 81–106.

Buchowski, Krzysztof. 2020. "The Pragmatic (Post-)Communist: Algirdas Brazauskas – the First Secretary, President, and Prime Minister of Lithuania." *Studia z Dziejów Rosji i Europy Środkowo-Wschodniej* 55 (3): 191.

Cirhan, Tomáš, and Petr Kopecký. 2020. "From Ideology to Interest-Driven Politics: Václav Klaus, Andrej Babiš and Two Eras of Party Leadership in the Czech Republic." In *Party Leaders in Eastern Europe: Personality, Behavior and Consequences*, edited by Sergiu Gherghina, 93–119. Cham: Palgrave Macmillan.

Grotz, Florian, Ferdinand Müller-Rommel, Jan Berz, Corinna Kroeber, and Marko Kukec. 2021. "How Political Careers Affect Prime-Ministerial Performance: Evidence from Central and Eastern Europe." *Comparative Political Studies* 54 (11): 1907–38.

Keudel-Kaiser, Dorothea. 2016. "Party System Factors and the Formation of Minority Governments in Central and Eastern Europe." *Zeitschrift Für Vergleichende Politikwissenschaft* 10 (3–4): 341–69.

Malová, Darina, and Tim Haughton. 2002. "Making Institutions in Central and Eastern Europe, and the Impact of Europe." *West European Politics* 25 (2): 101–20.

Strangio, Paul, Paul 't Hart, and James Walter. 2013. *Understanding Prime-Ministerial Performance: Comparative Perspectives*. Edited by Paul Strangio, Paul 't Hart, and James Walter. Oxford: Oxford University Press.

't Hart, Paul, and David Schelfhout. 2016. "Assessing Prime-Ministerial Performance in a Multiparty Democracy: The Dutch Case." *Acta Politica* 51 (2): 153–72.

Index

Note: **Bold** page numbers refer to tables; *italic* page numbers refer to figures and page numbers followed by "n" denote endnotes.

Adamkus, Valdas 70, 74, **75**
Agency for Bulgarians Abroad 46
Alternative for the Revival (ABV) of Bulgaria 43–45
ANO party 12
Ansip, Andrus 4, **5**
Antall, József 10
Ataka party 40–42, 44

Babiš, Andrej 12
Bajnai, Gordon 15, 51, 52, 55–64, **62**, 65n1, 65n4, 101
Basescu, Traian 84, 93–94
Baylis, Thomas A. 1–2, 85
Blair, Tony 58
bloc politics 52, 53, 56
Blue Coalition (SK) 40, 41
Boc, Emil 84, 94, 96
Borisov, Boyko 4, **5**, 11, 15, 35–48, 100–102
Boross, Péter 10
Bratušek, Alenka 11, 15, 21, 28–31, 100, 101
Brazauskas, Algirdas M. 4, 73–74
Bridge of Independent Lists 15, 21
Bulgaria, Borisov's survival in 35–48, **39**;
    Alternative for the Revival 43–45; assessment 38–46; battling ideological heterogeneity 43–44; behaviour of 38; challenges 36–38, 47–48; GERB performance in legislative elections 44–45, *45*; longevity 35, 46; National Council on Co-operation on Ethnic and Integration 45; new party within minority cabinet 39–42; parliamentary support 41–44, 46; personnel policy 40–41, 43–46; surprise resignation 42; Transparency International-Bulgarian Chapter 41; two years of streamlined coalition 44–46; unnecessary resignation 44; *see also* GERB party

Bulgarian Democratic Centre (BDC) 43
Bulgarian Socialist Party (BSP) 38, 41–43, 46, 48n7, 48n8

cabinet duration, in CEE democracies 1, **5**, 9, **9**; in Bulgaria **39**; by cabinet type and inclusion of GNPs **11**; comparative analysis of 101; in Croatia **24**; in Hungary **54**; in Lithuania **75**; in Romania **89**; in Slovenia **28**
cabinet: level 22, 23; performance, in Hungary 61–63; reshuffles 8, 23, 26, 27, 29–30, 41–43, 92
Cakar, Dario Nikic 15
Carey, John M. 12, 13
Central and Eastern Europe (CEE), PMs/party governments in 1–16; in Bulgaria 35–48, **39**; in Croatia 20–32, **24**; decision-making in democracies 2, 3; in Hungary 51–65, **54**; in Lithuania 69–82, **75**; longest-serving PMs 4–6, **5**; position of 2–6; in post-communist Romania 84–97, **89**, 99–104; in Slovenia 20–32, **28**
Cerar, Miro 11, 15, 21, 28–31, 100–102
Christian-Democratic National Peasants' Party 92
Christian Democratic People's Party 65n2
Christian democrats 9
Ciolos, Dacian 95
Ciorbea, Victor 92, 96
coalition: Croatia and Slovenia, prime-ministers in 20–32, **24**, **28**; formation process 10; HDZ-led 25; heterogeneous 15; intra-coalition conflicts 8, 22, 23, 25, 27, 31; minimal-winning 5, 24, 30; negotiation process 30; party leaders 22–23; viable 25
cohabitation 12–13, 81, 86–88, 102; croatian PMs under 14; formal 72–73; of presidents and PMs 12–13, **13**, 69; in semi-presidential regimes 103

108 INDEX

Communist Lithuanian Democratic Labour Party 74
confidence vote 42
conflict-management mechanisms 22, 23, 25, 29–31
conflict-resolution mechanisms 29
Constantinescu, Emil 84, 92–93
Constitutional Assembly 88
Constitutional Court 42
constructive opposition party 55
constructive vote of no-confidence (CVNC) 54, 57
contextual features, prime-ministers position 3–4, 6
Council for Cooperation 25
Croatian Democratic Union (HDZ) 14, 25–26, 100–102
Croatia, prime-ministerial survival 14, 20–32, **24**; bipolar structure of party competition 25; challenge for 21–22; conflict management mechanisms 22, 23, 25, 31; ethnic minority representatives 32n2; genuinely new parties 20–32; individual power resources 22, 23; patterns of 23–27; strategies of 21–23; success factors 27
Curini, Luigi 55

Dancila, Viorica 95
Democratic Coalition (DK) 59
Democratic Party of Pensioners of Slovenia (DeSUS) 30
democratic transition 27, 88
Democrats for Strong Bulgaria (DSB) 44
domestic policy 6, 77, 104
DPS *see* Movement for Rights and Freedoms (DPS)
Dragnea, Liviu 95
Drnovšek, Janez 4, **5**, 10, 27, 29
Dzurinda, Mikuláš **5**

early elections 9, 42, 44, 88, 93
economic transformation 2
Ekman, Joakim 85
electoral cycles 79–81, *79, 80*, 87
Europeanization: in Bulgaria 35–48, **39**; in Croatia 20–32, **24**; decision-making in democracies 2, 3; economic transformation and 2; in Hungary 51–65, **54**; in Lithuania 69–82, **75**; longest-serving PMs 4–6, **5**; PMs/party governments in 1–16; position of 2–6; in post-communist Romania 84–97, **89**, 99–104; in Slovenia 20–32, **28**
European Peoples' Party 40

Fico, Robert 4, **5**, 63
formal mechanisms, conflict management 22, 30, 31

fragile convergence 94
French cohabitation 87

genuinely new parties (GNPs) 10–12, 15, 36, 100–102; assumptions 23; in Croatia and Slovenia 20–32
GERB party 35, 43–44, 47, 48n9, 101–103; challenges 39; minority government 42; in national elections 40; parliamentary group of 41; performance in legislative elections 44–45, *45*; personnel policy 45–46; *see also* Bulgaria, Borissov's survival in
government policy 6, 40, 53, 69
Governor of Romania's National Bank 93
Grant National Assembly 48n3
Grecu, Razvan 91
Grindeanu, Sorin 95
Gross, Stanislav 9
Grotz, Florian 7, 22
Grybauskaitė, Dalia 74, **75**, 81
Gyurcsány, Ferenc 10, 15, 51, 52, 55–64, **62**, 65n1, 101–102

Haralampiev, Petar 46
HDZ *see* Croatian Democratic Union (HDZ)
Hino, Airo 55
Hungarian–Slovak relations 63
Hungarian Socialist Party (MSZP) 15, 51, 55–61, 64, 101
Hungary, prime-ministers in 51–65, **54**; bloc politics 52, 53, 56; case selection 54–57; centrist heuristics 56; crisis management 56; full technocratic government 60; government-initiated bills **62**; hyper-accountability cycles 57; measuring cabinet performance 61–63; measuring ideological position 58–61; minority cabinets 52–54; multilevel dynamics 56; neoliberal politics 58; policy performance 52–54; political career 57–58; simulated technocratic government 61

ideological proximity 52, 55, 64
Iliescu, Ion 91–92
Illés, Gábor 63
Ilonszki, Gabriella 65n5
individual-centred approach 21
individual power resources 22, 23
individual resources 3, 31
informal mechanisms, conflict management 22, 30, 31
intra-cabinet conflicts 22, 23, 57
intra-coalition conflicts 8, 22, 23, 25–27, 31
intra-executive competition 71
Iohannis, Klaus 84, 95–96
Isarescu, Mugur 93
Ivanov, Hristo 43

INDEX

109

Jankovic, Zoran 28–30, 100–101
Janša, Janez 4, **5**, 28, 29
Janša, Slovenian 21
Jastramskis, Mažvydas 15, 103

Kaczynski, Jaroslaw 8
Kalfin, Ivaylo 44
Karamarko, Tomislav 25, 26
KDNP *see* Christian Democratic People's Party
Klaus, Vacláv 4
Klüver, Heike 52
Köker, Philipp 71
Kolarova, Rumyana 48n2
Körösényi, András 63
Kovacheva, Diana 41
Kovarek, Daniel 15, 101
Krašovec, Alenka 15, 29, 100, 102
Krpič, Tomaž 29
Krzaklewski, Marian 8
Kubilius, Andrius 4

lack of convergence 94
Law and Justice Party (PiS) 8
legislative process 12–13
Liberal-Democratic Party (PDL) 91
List of Zoran Jankovic–Positive Slovenia (LZJ-PS) 15, 21, 28
Lithuania, prime-ministers in 69–82, **75**; bivariate statistics 75; case of 73–74; data and methods 74–75; electoral cycles 79–80, *79, 80*; intra-executive conflict 70; mixed-method approach 74; parliamentary support **76**, 76–79, **77**; presidential activism 70–81, **76, 77**, *79, 80*, 82n1; results 75–80; selection in parliamentary systems 70; semi-presidential systems 70–73; strong and weak institutionalised parties 78

majority government 91, 103; preponderance of 54; single-party 5; *see also* minority government
McDonnell, Duncan 60
MDF 52, 55, 56, 62–64, 65n3
Meciar, Vladimír 4, **5**
Medgyessy, Péter 10, 57
Milanović 24, 25, 32n3
minimal-winning coalitions 5, 24, 30
Minister of Finance 26
Minister of Local Government and Regional Development 57
Minister of the Judiciary 43
Ministry of Youth Affairs and Sports 57
minority government 9, 38, 86, 104; cabinets 3; GERB 42; HDZ-led coalition 25; in Hungary case 15, 51–65, 101; prime ministers in 51–65; single-party 4; status 10; *see also* majority government

Most party 24–27, 31, 100–102
Movement for Rights and Freedoms (DPS) 41–42, 46, 48n8
MSSD framework 51, 56, 61, 64
MSZP *see* Hungarian Socialist Party (MSZP)
multilevel dynamics 52, 56
multi-party governments 8, 23

Nastase, Adrian 92
National Assembly 42, 43, 46, 48n9, 55, 56, 61, **62**, 64
National Council on Co-operation on Ethnic and Integration 45
National Movement Simeon the Second (NDSV) 38–40, 48n8
national politics 23, 27, 35, 39, 47
National Salvation Front (FSN) 91
NDSV *see* National Movement Simeon the Second (NDSV)
Necas, Petr 12
new party 10; challenge 20–32; electoral potential of 25; Živi zid 24–25; within minority cabinet 39–42; Most 24–27, 31, 100–102
Nikic-Cakar, Dario 100, 102

opposition parties 3, 10, 12, 14, 26; in Bulgaria 38, 41; in Croatia and Slovenia 26; in Hungary 52, 53, 55, 56, 61; in Romania 86, 87, 93, 94, 96, 97
Orban, Ludovic 96
Orbán, Viktor 4, **5**
Order, Law and Justice Party (RZS) 40–42
Oreškovic, Tihomir 15, 21, 24–27, 31, 32n4, 100

Pahor 21, 29
parliamentary system 1–2; Borissov's survival 41–44, 46; Lithuania, prime-ministers in **76**, 76–79, **77**; parties 8–12; political executives in 2–3; state presidents in 3
Paroubek, Jirí 9
partisan congruence **13**, 13–15, 102–103
Parts, Juhan 11
party: affiliations 3, 69, **89–90**; coalition level 22, 23
party governments, in CEE 1–16; in Bulgaria 35–48, **39**; comparative study 1; in Croatia 20–32, **24**; in Hungary 51–65, **54**; in Lithuania 69–82, **75**; position 2–6; in post-communist Romania 84–97, **89**, 99–104; in Slovenia 20–32, **28**; stable and effective 1
party leaders 6–8, **7**, 14, 38, 99–101; coalition 22–23; conflict-management mechanism 29; effective 23, 31; intra-coalition conflicts 25; in policy-making process 26; and political experience 22–23; in Romania 88

passive reshuffles 8
Pastorella, Giulia 60
Patriotic Front (PF) 43, 44
PDL *see* Liberal-Democratic Party (PDL)
personal conflicts 29, 30, 100
personnel policy, Borissov's survival 40–41, 43–46
Petrov, Božo 25, 26
PiS *see* Law and Justice Party (PiS)
Plenković, Andrej 15, 21, 24, 25, 27, 31, 32n4, 100, 101
policy-making process 26
policy performance, in Hungary 51–56, 60, 63, 64
political: career, in Hungary 57–58; conflicts 3, 13, 69; convergence 86, 93–94
political party 2–3, 6, 77, 81, 92–93; activities in 73; Croatian purification 25
Ponta, Victor 94, 96
Pope John Paul II 59
Popescu-Tariceanu, Calin 93, 96
positional agenda power 52, 55
post-communist democracies, prime ministers 1, 4, 6; argument on extraordinary difficult 4; multi-party cabinets in 8; parties, parliaments and presidents 99–104; political actors in 3; political convergence 86; presidential powers in 14; in Romania 84–97, **89**; stability of 2, 10
presidential activism 15, 70–81, **76**, **77**, *79*, *80*, 82n1; categories of explanatory factors 71–72; Seimas elections 73, 78, *79*; strength score and **77**; success of 74–75; weakness score and instances of **76**
prime-ministers (PMs), in CEE 1–16; in Bulgaria 35–48, **39**; concrete mechanisms 100; constitutional design 99; contextual features 3–4; in Croatia 20–32, **24**; in Hungary 51–65, **54**; implications to maintain position 3; institutional and political context 99; in Lithuania 69–82, **75**; longest-serving 4–6, **5**; longevity 3; parliamentary parties 8–12; partisanship congruence **13**, 13–15, 102–103; party leadership 6–8, **7**; performance 3, 100, 104; in post-communist Romania 84–97, **89**, 99–104; in Slovenia 20–32, **28**; strategies of 21–23; strength of 3
Protsyk, Oleh 86
PSD *see* Social Democratic Party (PSD)
Public Affairs party 12
Pukelis, Lukas 15, 103

Racan 25, 32n3
Raunio, Tapio 69, 71, 74
Raykov, Marin 42
Reform Alliance 62

reform economists 60
Reformers' Block (RB) 43, 45
resignation, Borissov's survival 42, 44
Romanian Constitution 88
Romanian Democratic Convention (CDR) 92
Romania, post-communist 84–97, **89**; empirical analysis 91–96; semi-presidentialism 88, **89–90**, 91
Russinova, Zornitsa 44
RZS *see* Order, Law and Justice Party (RZS)

Sanader, Ivo **5**, 10, 25
Šarec, Marjan 27, 28
Saxecoburggotski, Simeon 11, 38–39, 46, 47, 48n5, 48n6
SDS *see* Union of Democratic Forces (SDS)
Sedelius, Thomas 69, 71, 74, 85
semi-presidential systems 1, 69; competition over ministerial selection in 70–73; political conflict in 69; research on 70; Romanian 85–88, **89–90**, 91
Sharenkova-Toshkova, Radostina 15, 100, 102
Shugart, Matthew Søberg 12, 13
Simeonov, Valeri 45
Simonovits, András 62
simulated technocratic government 61
single-member districts (SMDs) 56
single-party governments 40, 53, 55, 64; majorities in parliamentary democracies 3; minority *vs.* majority governments 4–5; rule 23; in Westminster democracies 8
Sitter, Nick 60, 62
Skvernelis cabinet 78, 81
Slovenian Democratic Party (SDP) 29
Slovenia, prime-ministers in 20–32, **28**; conflict-management mechanisms 29–31; constitutional framework 27; fiscal and financial system 29–30; genuinely new parties 20–32; patterns of 27–30; strategies of 21–23
snap elections 55, 56, 58
Sobotka, Bohuslav 12
Social Democratic Party (PSD) 88, 91
Social Democrats (SD) 9, 30
Social-Liberal Union (USL) 94
socioeconomic context 4
Solidarity Electoral Action 8
Špidla, Vladimír 9
Spirova, Maria 15, 48n2, 100, 102
splinter 25, 36, 43, 57, 59, 94, 95
state presidents 12–14, **13**, 102–103; constitutional powers of 13; impact 85; in parliamentary systems 3; partisanship of 4
Stefan, Laurentiu 16, 65n5, 91, 103
Stolojan, Theodor 91

INDEX

streamlined coalition, Borissov's survival 44–46
strong convergence 86, 96
SZDSZ 15, 51, 52, 55–64, 101–102

Tanov, Vanyo 42
technocrats 8, 60, 91, 92, 94; cabinets 72, 76, **76**, 78, 86, 100; government 60, 61, 64, 95; independent 25; predecessor 101
Tenev, Pavel 45
Third Way approach 58
three-party government 10, 12, 41
Török, Gábor 60
Tóth, Csaba 60
Troika 29
Tudose, Mihai 95
Tusk, Donald 4, **5**

Ungureanu, Mihai Razvan 84, 94, 96
Union of Democratic Forces (SDS) 38
USL *see* Social-Liberal Union (USL)

Vacaroiu, Nicolae 92, 96
Vagnorius, Gediminas 70
Valbruzzi, Marco 60
Vasile, Radu 84, 92
Volya 46, 48n9

weak convergence 86, 93–94, 96
Weber, Till 7, 22

Zhivkov, Todor 39
Živi zid (Human Shield) 24–25
Zubek, Radoslaw 52

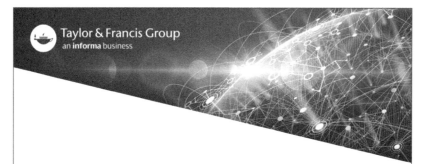